NEVADA 30-HOUR APPLIED REAL ESTATE PRACTICES COURSE

AN INTERACTIVE PROGRAM FOR SALEPERSONS

PERFORMANCE
PROGRAMS
COMPANY

Stephen Mettling
David Cusic
Ben Schéible

Material in this book is not intended to represent legal advice and should not be so construed. Readers should consult legal counsel for advice regarding points of law.

© 2022 by Performance Programs Company
502 S. Fremont Ave., Suite 724, Tampa, FL 33606
info@performanceprogramscompany.com
www.performanceprogramscompany.com

ISBN: 978-1955919128

Nevada 30-Hour Applied Real Estate Practices Course

Table of Contents

Nevada 30-Hour Applied Real Estate Practices Course

Course Overview

The content of this course covers essential contract law, both national and Nevada-specific, and the laws of agency, likewise both national and specific to Nevada. In addition, and along related lines, the program presents a terse review of the issues defining and impacting the broker – sales associate relationship. The program ends with a comprehensive survey of risk management and how to manage risk minimization in your brokerage practice, particularly in contexts that impact contracts, agency, and activities within the brokerage.

As a format preview, this course is comprised of seven chapters. Each chapter begins with an informative text narrative summarizing key points of required content. Subsequently, participants will be given quiz questions following each chapter. Following Chapter 3 and Chapter 7, students will engage in a skills workshop focusing on conveyance contracts and brokerage agreements, respectively. Students will be required to participate by answering problem-solving questions and situations.

The intent of these chapters, and the program as a whole, is to give students an interactive opportunity to focus on the day-to-day skills of contracting, working with clients, and managing one's practice so that such practice can be delivered in a professional manner and in full compliance with Nevada's many underlying laws and regulations.

ABOUT THE AUTHORS

For nearly fifty years, Stephen Mettling has been actively engaged in real estate education. Beginning with Dearborn in 1972, then called Real Estate Education Company, Mr. Mettling managed the company's textbook division and author acquisitions. Subsequently he built up the company's real estate school division which eventually became the country's largest real estate, insurance and securities school network in the country. In 1978, Mr. Mettling founded Performance Programs Company, a custom training program publishing and development company specializing in commercial, industrial, and corporate real estate. Over time, Performance Programs Company narrowed its focus to real estate textbook and exam prep publishing. Currently the Company's texts and prelicense resources are used in hundreds of schools in over 48 states. Mr. Mettling has authored over 100 textbooks, real estate programs and exam prep manuals.

Mr. Cusic, an author and educator with international real estate training experience, has been engaged in vocation-oriented education since 1966. Specializing in real estate training since 1983, he has developed numerous real estate training programs for corporate and institutional clients around the country.

Ben Scheible is a licensed real estate broker-salesperson in Nevada, and a licensed real estate broker and attorney in California. He practiced real estate law for 15 years before becoming a full time educator and consultant. Stanford University graduate, real estate author, attorney, national speaker, and expert witness in real estate law, he has published a number of real estate books including Nevada Real Estate License Exam Prep. Ben has also developed more than 100 approved CE courses and conducted over 1,000 seminars and workshops.

SECTION 1 – REAL ESTATE CONTRACTS

Chapter 1:
Fundamentals of Contract Law

Real estate contracts are the legal agreements that underlie the transfer and financing of real estate, as well as the real estate brokerage business. Sale and lease contracts and option agreements are used to transfer real estate interests from one party to another. Mortgage contracts and promissory agreements are part of financing real estate. Listing and representation contracts establish client relationships and provide for compensation.

In order to work with real estate contracts, it is imperative first to grasp basic concepts that apply to all contracts in general. These concepts provide a foundation for understanding the specifics of particular types of real estate contract.

VALIDITY AND ENFORCEABILITY OF CONTRACTS

A **contract** is an agreement between two or more parties who, in a "meeting of the minds," have pledged to perform or refrain from performing some act. A *valid* contract is one that is *legally enforceable* by virtue of meeting certain requirements of contract law. If a contract does not meet the requirements, it is not valid and the parties to it cannot resort to a court of law to enforce its provisions.

Note that a contract is not a legal form or a prescribed set of words in a document, but rather the intangible agreement that was made in "the meeting of the minds" of the parties to the contract.

Legal status of contracts

In terms of validity and enforceability, a court may construe the legal status of a contract in one of four ways:

> ▸ valid
> ▸ valid but unenforceable
> ▸ void
> ▸ voidable

Valid. A valid contract is one which meets the legal requirements for validity. These requirements are explained in the next section.

A valid contract that is in writing is enforceable within a statutory time period. A valid contract that is made orally is also generally enforceable within a statutory period, with the exceptions noted below.

Valid but unenforceable. State laws declare that some contracts are enforceable only if they are in writing. These laws apply in particular to the transfer of interests in real estate. Thus, while an oral contract may meet the tests for validity, if it falls under the laws requiring a written contract, the parties will not have legal recourse to enforce performance. An oral long-term lease and an oral real estate sales contract are examples of contracts that may be valid but not enforceable.

Note that such contracts, if valid, remain so even though not enforceable. This means that if the parties fully execute and perform the contract, the outcome may not be altered.

Void. A void contract is an agreement that does not meet the tests for validity, and therefore is no contract at all. If a contract is void, neither party can enforce it.

For example, a contract that does not include consideration is void. Likewise, a contract to extort money from a business is void. Void contracts and instruments are also described as "null and void."

Voidable. A voidable contract is one which initially appears to be valid, but is subject to rescission by a party to the contract who is deemed to have acted under some kind of disability. Only the party who claims the disability may rescind the legal effect of the contract.

For example, a party who was the victim of duress, coercion, or fraud in creation of a contract, and can prove it, may disaffirm the contract. However, the disaffirmation must occur within a legal time frame for the act of rescission to be valid. Similarly, if the party who has cause to disaffirm the contract elects instead to perform it, the contract is no longer voidable but valid.

A voidable contract differs from a void contract in that the latter does not require an act of disaffirmation to render it unenforceable.

Criteria for validity

A contract is valid only if it meets all of the following criteria:

- **competent parties**
- **mutual consent**
- **valuable consideration**
- **legal purpose**
- **voluntary, good faith act**

Competent parties. The parties to a contract must have the capacity to contract, and there must be at least two such parties. Thus, the owner of a tenancy for life cannot deed his interest to himself in the form of a fee simple, as this would involve only one party. Capacity to contract is determined by three factors:

- ▸ legal age
- ▸ mental competency
- ▸ legitimate authority

Depending on state law, a contract involving a minor as a party may be either void or voidable. If the law allows a minor to contract, the contract will generally be voidable and the minor can disaffirm the contract.

To be mentally competent, a party must have sufficient understanding of the import and consequences of a contract. Competency in this context is separate and distinct from sanity. Incompetent parties, or parties of "unsound mind," may not enter into enforceable contracts. The incompetency of a party may be ruled by a court of law or by other means. In some areas, convicted felons may be deemed incompetent, depending on the nature of the crime.

During the period of one's incompetency, a court may appoint a guardian who may act on the incompetent party's behalf with court approval.

If the contracting party is representing another person or business entity, the representative must have the *legal authority* to contract. If representing another person, the party must have a bona fide power of attorney. If the contracting party is representing a corporation, the person must have the appropriate power and approval to act, such as would be conferred in a duly executed resolution of the Board of Directors. If the contracting entity is a general partnership, any partner may validly contract for the partnership. In a limited partnership, only general partners may be parties to a contract.

Mutual consent. Mutual consent, also known as *offer and acceptance* and *meeting of the minds,* requires that a contract involve a clear and definite offer and an intentional, unqualified acceptance of the offer. In effect, the parties must agree to the terms without equivocation. A court may nullify a contract where the acceptance of terms by either party was partial, accidental, or vague.

Valuable consideration. A contract must contain a two-way exchange of valuable consideration as compensation for performance by the other party. The exchange of considerations must be two-way. The contract is not valid or enforceable if just one party provides consideration.

Valuable consideration can be something of tangible value, such as money or something a party promises to do or not do. For example, a home builder may promise to build a house for a party as consideration for receiving money from the home buyer. Or, a landowner may agree not to sell a property as consideration for a developer's option money. Also, valuable consideration can be something intangible that a party must give up, such as a homeowner's occupancy of the house in exchange for rent. In effect, consideration is the price one party must pay to obtain performance from the other party.

Valuable consideration may be contrasted with good consideration, or "love and affection," which does not qualify as consideration in a valid contract. Good consideration is something of questionable value, such as a child's love for her mother. Good consideration disqualifies a contract because, while one's love or affection is certainly valuable to the other party, it is not something that is specifically offered in exchange for something else. Good consideration can, however, serve as a nominal consideration in transferring a real property interest as a gift.

In some cases, what is promised as valuable consideration must also be deemed to be *sufficient* consideration. Grossly insufficient consideration, such as $50,000 for a $2 million property, may invalidate a contract on the grounds that the agreement is a gift rather than a contract. In other cases where there is an extreme imbalance in the considerations exchanged, a contract may be invalidated as a violation of good faith bargaining.

Legal purpose. The content, promise, or intent of a contract must be lawful. A contract that proposes an illegal act is void.

Voluntary, good faith act. The parties must create the contract in good faith as a free and voluntary act. A contract is thus voidable if one party acted under duress, coercion, fraud, or misrepresentation.

For example, if a property seller induces a buyer to purchase a house based on assurances that the roof is new, the buyer may rescind the agreement if the roof turns out to be twenty years old and leaky.

Validity of a conveyance contract

In addition to satisfying the foregoing general contract validity requirements, a contract that *conveys an interest in real estate* must:

- ▶ be in writing
- ▶ contain a legal description of the property
- ▶ be signed by one or more of the parties

A lease contract that has a term of one year or less is an exception. Such leases do not have to be in writing to be enforceable.

Enforcement limitations

Certain contracts that fail to meet the validity requirements are voidable if a damaged party takes appropriate action. The enforcement of voidable contracts, however, is limited by **statutes of limitation**. Certain other contracts which are valid may not be enforceable due to the **statute of frauds**.

Statute of limitations. The statute of limitations restricts the time period for which an injured party in a contract has the right to rescind or disaffirm the contract. A party to a voidable contract must act within the statutory period.

Statute of frauds. The statute of frauds requires that certain contracts *must be in writing* to be enforceable. Real estate contracts that convey an interest in real property fall in this category, with the exception that a lease of one year's duration or less may be oral. All other contracts to buy, sell, exchange, or lease interests in real property must be in writing to be enforceable. In addition, *exclusive listing agreements* in most states must be in writing.

The statute of frauds concerns the enforceability of a contract, not its validity. Once the parties to a valid oral contract have executed and performed it, even if the contract was unenforceable, a party cannot use the Statute of Frauds to rescind the contract.

For example, a broker and a seller have an oral agreement. Following the terms of the agreement, the broker finds a buyer, and the seller pays the commission. They have now executed the contract, and the seller cannot later force the broker to return the commission based on the statute of frauds.

Electronic contracting

Contracting electronically via email and fax greatly facilitates the completion of transactions. Clients, lenders, title agents, inspectors, brokers, and other participants in a transaction can quickly share documentation and information. Electronic contracting is made possible by the Uniform Electronic Transactions Act (UETA) and the Electronic Signatures in Global and National Commerce Act (E-Sign), which are federal laws. UETA, which has been accepted in most states, provides that electronic records and signatures are legal and must be accepted. E-Sign makes contracts, records, and signatures legally enforceable, regardless of medium, even where UETA is not accepted.

CONTRACT CREATION

Offer and acceptance

The mutual consent required for a valid contract is reached through the process of offer and acceptance: The **offeror** proposes contract terms in an **offer** to the **offeree**. If the offeree accepts all terms without amendment, the offer becomes a contract. The exact point at which the offer becomes a contract is when the offeree gives the offeror notice of the acceptance.

Offer. An offer expresses the offeror's intention to enter into a contract with an offeree to perform the terms of the agreement in exchange for the offeree's performance. In a real estate sale or lease contract, the offer must clearly contain all intended terms of the contract in writing and be communicated to the offeree.

If an offer contains an expiration date and the phrase "time is of the essence," the offer expires at exactly the time specified. In the absence of a stated time period, the offeree has a "reasonable" time to accept an offer.

Acceptance. An offer gives the offeree the power of accepting. For an acceptance to be valid, the offeree must manifestly and unequivocally accept all terms of the offer without change, and so indicate by signing the offer, preferably with a date of signing. The acceptance must then be communicated to the offeror. If the communication of acceptance is by mail, the offer is considered to be communicated as soon as it is placed in the mail.

Counteroffer

By changing any of the terms of an offer, the offeree creates a counteroffer, and the original offer is void. At this point, the offeree becomes the offeror, and the new offeree gains the right of acceptance. If accepted, the counteroffer becomes a valid contract provided all other requirements are met.

For example, a seller changes the expiration date of a buyer's offer by one day, signs the offer and returns it to the buyer. The single amendment extinguishes the buyer's offer, and the buyer is no longer bound by any agreement. The seller's amended offer is a counteroffer which now gives the buyer the right of acceptance. If the buyer accepts the counteroffer, the counteroffer becomes a binding contract.

Revocation of an offer

An offer may be revoked, or withdrawn, at any time before the offeree has communicated acceptance. The revocation extinguishes the offer and the offeree's right to accept it.

For example, a buyer has offered to purchase a house for the listed price. Three hours later, a family death radically changes the buyer's plans. She immediately calls the seller and revokes the offer, stating she is no longer interested in the house. Since the seller had not communicated acceptance of the offer to the buyer, the offer is legally cancelled.

If the offeree has paid consideration to the offeror to leave an offer open, and the offeror accepts, an option has been created which cancels the offeror's right to revoke the offer over the period of the option.

Termination of an offer

Any of the following actions or circumstances can terminate an offer:

- acceptance: the offeree accepts the offer, converting it to a contract
- rejection: the offeree rejects the offer
- revocation: the offeror withdraws the offer before acceptance
- lapse of time: the offer expires
- counteroffer: the offeree changes the offer
- death or insanity of either party

Assignment of a contract

A real estate contract *that is not a personal contract for services* can be assigned to another party unless the terms of the agreement specifically prohibit assignment.

Listing agreements, for example, are not assignable, since they are personal service agreements between agent and principal. Sales contracts, however, are assignable, because they involve the purchase of real property rather than a personal service.

Contract preparation

State laws define the extent to which real estate brokers and agents may legally prepare real estate contracts. Such laws, referred to as "broker-lawyer accords," also define what types of contracts brokers and agents may prepare. In Nevada, brokers and agents may not draft contracts, but they may use standard promulgated forms and complete the blanks in the form.

As a rule, a broker or agent who completes real estate contracts is engaging in the unauthorized practice of law unless the broker is a party to the agreement, such a listing agreement or sales contract. Brokers and agents may not complete leases, mortgages, contracts for deed, or promissory notes to which they are not a party.

Agents must be fully aware of what they are legally allowed to do and not do in preparing and interpreting contracts for clients in Nevada. In addition to practicing law without a license, agents expose themselves to lawsuits from clients who relied on a contract as being legally acceptable.

CLASSIFICATIONS OF CONTRACTS

Oral vs. written

A contract may be in writing or it may be an oral, or **parol**, contract. Certain oral contracts are valid and enforceable, others are not enforceable, even if valid. For example, most states require listing agreements, sales contracts, and leases exceeding one year to be in writing to be enforceable.

Express vs. implied

An **express contract** is one in which all the terms and covenants of the agreement have been manifestly stated and agreed to by all parties, whether verbally or in writing.

An **implied contract** is an unstated or unintentional agreement that may be deemed to exist when the *actions of any of the parties* suggest the existence of an agreement.

A common example of an implied contract is an implied agency agreement. In implied agency, an agent who does not have a contract with a buyer performs acts on the buyer's behalf, such as negotiating a price that is less than the listing price. In so doing, the agent has possibly created an implied contract with the buyer, albeit unintended. If the buyer compensates the agent for the negotiating efforts, the existence of an implied agency agreement becomes even less disputable.

Bilateral vs. unilateral

A **bilateral contract** is one in which both parties promise to perform their respective parts of an agreement in exchange for performance by the other party.

An example of a bilateral contract is an exclusive listing: the broker promises to exercise due diligence in the efforts to sell a property, and the seller promises to compensate the broker when and if the property sells.

In a **unilateral contract**, only one party promises to do something, provided the other party does something. The latter party is not obligated to perform any act, but the promising party must fulfill the promise if the other party chooses to perform.

An option is an example of a unilateral contract: in an option-to-buy, the party offering the option (optionor) promises to sell a property if the optionee decides to exercise the option. While the potential buyer does not have to buy, the owner must sell if the option is exercised.

Executed vs. executory

An **executed contract** is one that has been fully performed and fulfilled: neither party bears any further obligation. A completed and expired lease contract is an executed contract: the landlord may re-possess the premises and the tenant has no further obligation to pay rent.

An **executory contract** is one in which performance is yet to be completed. A sales contract prior to closing is executory: while the parties have agreed to buy and sell, the buyer has yet to pay the seller and the seller has yet to deed the property to the buyer.

CONTRACT TERMINATION

Forms of contract termination

Termination of a contract, also called **cancellation** and **discharge**, may occur for any of the following causes.

Performance. A contract terminates when fully performed by the parties. It may also terminate for:

> ▶ partial performance, if the parties agree
> ▶ sufficient performance, if a court determines a party has sufficiently performed the contract, even though not to the full extent of every provision

Infeasibility. An otherwise valid contract can be canceled if it is not possible to perform. Certain personal services contracts, for example, depend on the unique capabilities of one person which cannot be substituted by someone else. If such a person dies or is sufficiently disabled, the contract is cancelable.

Mutual agreement. Parties to a contract can agree to terminate, or renounce, the contract. If the parties wish to create a new contract to replace the cancelled contract, they must comply with the validity requirements for the new contract. Such substitution is called **novation**.

Cooling-period rescission. Rescission is the act of nullifying a contract. In many states, parties to certain contracts are allowed a statutory amount of time after entering into a contract, or "cooling period", to rescind the contract without cause. No reason need be stated for the cancellation, and the cancelling party incurs no liability for performance.

For example, consider the unsuspecting buyer of a lot in a new resort development. Such buyers are often the targets of hard-sell tactics which lead to a completed sales contract and a deposit. The statutory cooling period gives the buyer an opportunity to reconsider the investment in the absence of the persistent salesperson.

Revocation. Revocation is cancellation of the contract by one party without the consent of the other. For example, a seller may revoke a listing to take the property off the market. While all parties have the *power* to revoke, they may not have a defensible *right*. In the absence of justifiable grounds, a revocation may not relieve the revoking party of contract obligations.

For example, a seller who revokes a listing without grounds may be required to pay a commission if the broker found a buyer or reimburse the broker's marketing expenses if no buyer was found.

Abandonment. Abandonment occurs when parties fail to perform contract obligations. This situation may allow the parties to cancel the contract.

Lapse of time. If a contract contains an expiration provision and date, the contract automatically expires on the deadline.

Invalidity of contract. If a contract is void, it terminates without the need for disaffirmation. A voidable contract can be cancelled by operation of law or by rescission.

Breach of contract

A breach of contract is a failure to perform according to the terms of the agreement. Also called **default**, a breach of contract gives the damaged party the right to take legal action.

The damaged party may elect the following legal remedies:

  ▶ rescission
  ▶ forfeiture
  ▶ suit for damages
  ▶ suit for specific performance

Rescission. A damaged party may rescind the contract. This cancels the contract and returns the parties to their pre-contract condition, including the refunding of any monies already transferred.

Forfeiture. A forfeiture requires the breaching party to give up something, according to the terms of the contract. For example, a buyer who defaults on a sales contract may have to forfeit the earnest money deposit.

Suit for damages. A damaged party may sue for money damages in civil court. The suit must be initiated within the time period allowed by the statute of limitations. When a contract states the total amount due to a damaged party in the event of a breach, the compensation is known as **liquidated damages**. If the contract does not specify the amount, the damaged party may sue in court for **unliquidated damages**.

Suit for specific performance. A suit for specific performance is an attempt to force the defaulting party to comply with the terms of the contract. Specific performance suits occur when it is difficult to identify damages because of the unique circumstances of the real property in question. The most common instance is a defaulted sale or lease contract where the buyer or seller wants the court to compel the defaulting party to go through with the transaction, even when the defaulter would prefer to pay a damage award.

Check Your Understanding Quiz:

Chapter 1: Fundamentals of Contract Law

Carefully read each question and provide your best answer based on what you learned in this module. Then check your answers against the Answer Key which immediately follows the quiz questions.

1. Which of the following is NOT a requirement for a valid contract?

    a. Legally competent parties
    b. Valuable consideration
    c. A legal purpose
    d. It must be objectively fair to both parties.

2. The statute of frauds

    a. requires certain contracts to be in writing to be enforceable.
    b. establishes the time limit within which a lawsuit must be filed.
    c. invalidates a contract that was entered through fraud.
    d. establishes the minimum consideration required for a legal contract.

3. Ron agreed to sell a house to Maria. Shortly before the close of escrow, Ron announced that he would not deliver title to Maria. Here, the statute of limitations

    a. specifies that Maria does not have a remedy unless the agreement was in writing.
    b. specifies how long Maria must wait before filing a lawsuit.
    c. specifies how long Maria has to file a lawsuit.
    d. specifies the maximum amount Maria can recover.

4. Dave offered to buy Barbara's house for $675,000. Barbara made a counteroffer to sell for $700,000 but has regrets about it. Can Barbara legally revoke the counteroffer and accept Dave's offer for $675,000 if time has not expired on the offer?

    a. Yes.
    b. No, Barbara's counteroffer extinguished Dave's offer.
    c. No, Dave's offer is not enough.
    d. Yes, if Barbara revokes the counteroffer before Dave acts on it.

5. Jose made an offer to buy Martha's house, specifying that the offer would remain open until June 20, 20__. On June 18, 20__, Jose sent an email to Martha stating "Things have changed for me, and I am revoking my offer to buy your house. /s/ Jose." What is the status of this transaction?

    a. Martha can still accept the offer because the time has not expired.
    b. Jose has successfully revoked the offer and the transaction is terminated.
    c. Martha can still accept the offer because it cannot be revoked with an email.
    d. It cannot be determined without knowing how much Jose offered.

6. Which of the following most accurately defines a contract?

   a. It is a legally enforceable agreement.
   b. It is an understanding.
   c. It is an agreement put into writing.
   d. It is an agreement to do or refrain doing something.

7. In which of the following types of contracts may one party choose to affirm and enforce the agreement, or choose to disaffirm the contract?

   a. A void contract
   b. A voidable contract
   c. An unenforced contract
   d. A unilateral contract

8. Which of the following is NOT a criterion for a valid contract?

   a. Competent parties
   b. A legal purpose
   c. Written by an attorney
   d. Valuable consideration

9. The mutual assent to form a contract is sometimes called

   a. a meeting of the minds.
   b. acquiescence.
   c. required consent.
   d. consensus.

10. Entering a contract through electronic means, for example via email, is generally

    a. unacceptable.
    b. acceptable if the parties agree.
    c. acceptable if proper encryption is used.
    d. acceptable if approved by the Real Estate Division.

11. Fred offered to buy Amy's house for $450,000, in including all necessary terms and conditions. Amy said she would "sell for $500,000." Fred said, "No". Amy said, "OK, I accept the original offer for $450,000." What is the status of negotiations?

    a. Fred and Amy have a contract.
    b. Fred and Amy do not have a contract because there is no accepted offer.
    c. Fred and Amy have a contract for $475,000.
    d. Fred and Amy have a contract for an unspecified amount.

12. The effective date of a contract is the date the

    a. offeree accepts the offer or counteroffer.
    b. offer is delivered to the offeree.
    c. offeree delivers an acceptance to the offeror.
    d. the date the offer expires if it is not rejected.

13. A contract to purchase real estate generally,

    a. cannot be assigned because it is a contract for personal services.
    b. cannot be assigned unless the contract specifically allows assignments.
    c. can be assigned unless the contract specifically prohibits assignments.
    d. can be assigned even if language in the contract prohibits assignments.

14. A liquidated damages clause in a real estate purchase contract

    a. specifies exactly how much the non-defaulting party will recover in the event of a default.
    b. specifies the maximum but not the minimum amount the non-defaulting will recover in the event of a default.
    c. specifies the minimum but not the maximum amount non-defaulting party will recover in the event of a default.
    d. Obligates a buyer to seek specific enforcement in the event of a seller default.

Answer Key:

Chapter 1: Fundamentals of Contract Law

1. d. It must be objectively fair to both parties.

2. a. requires certain contracts to be in writing to be enforceable.

3. c. specifies how long Maria has to file a lawsuit.

4. b. No, Barbara's counteroffer extinguished Dave's offer.

5. b. Jose has successfully revoked the offer and the transaction is terminated.

6. d. It is an agreement to do or refrain doing something

7. b. A voidable contract

8. c. Written by an attorney

9. a. a meeting of the minds

10. b. acceptable if the parties agree.

11. b. Fred and Amy do not have a contract because there is no accepted offer.

12. c. offeree delivers an acceptance to the offeror.

13. c. can be assigned unless the contract specifically prohibits assignments.

14. a. specifies exactly how much the non-defaulting party will recover in the event of a default.

Chapter 2:
Overview of Conveyance Contracts

CONTRACTS FOR SALE

A real estate sale contract is a binding and enforceable agreement wherein a buyer, the **vendee**, agrees to buy an identified parcel of real estate, and a seller, the **vendor**, agrees to sell it under certain terms and conditions. It is the document that is at the center of the transaction.

The conventional transfer of real estate ownership takes place in three stages. First, there is the negotiating period where buyers and sellers exchange offers in an effort to agree to all transfer terms that will appear in the sale contract. Second, when both parties have accepted all terms, the offer becomes a binding sale contract and the transaction enters the pre-closing stage, during which each party makes arrangements to complete the sale according to the sale contract's terms. Third is the closing of the transaction, when the seller deeds title to the buyer, the buyer pays the purchase price, and all necessary documents are completed. At this stage, the sale contract has served its purpose and terminates.

Other names for the sale contract are *agreement of sale, contract for purchase, contract of purchase and sale*, and *earnest money contract.*

Legal characteristics

Executory contract. A sale contract is *executory:* the signatories have yet to perform their respective obligations and promises. Upon closing, the sale contract is fully performed and no longer exists as a binding agreement.

Signatures. All owners of the property should sign the sale contract. If the sellers are married, both spouses should sign to ensure that both spouses release homestead, dower, and curtesy rights to the buyer at closing. Failure to do so does not invalidate the contract but can lead to encumbered title and legal disputes.

Enforceability criteria. To be enforceable, a sale contract must:

- be validly created (mutual consent, consideration, legal purpose, competent parties, voluntary act)
- be in writing
- identify the principal parties
- clearly identify the property, preferably by legal description
- contain a purchase price
- be signed by the principal parties

Written vs. oral form. A contract for the sale of real estate is enforceable only if it is in writing. A buyer or seller cannot sue to force the other to comply with an oral contract for sale, even if the contract is valid.

Assignment. Either party to a sale transaction can assign the sale contract to another party, subject to the provisions and conditions contained in the agreement.

Who may complete. A broker or agent may assist buyer and seller in completing an offer to purchase, provided the broker represents the client faithfully and does not charge a separate fee for the assistance. It is advisable, and legally required in most states (including Nevada), for a broker to use a standard contract form promulgated by state agencies or real estate boards, as such forms contain generally accepted language. This relieves the broker of the dangers of creating new contract language, which can be construed as a practice of law for which the broker is not licensed.

Contract creation

Offer and acceptance. A contract of sale is created by full and unequivocal acceptance of an offer. Offer and acceptance may come from either buyer or seller. The offeree must accept the offer without making any changes whatsoever. A change terminates the offer and creates a new offer, or counteroffer. An offeror may revoke an offer for any reason prior to communication of acceptance by the offeree.

Equitable title. A sale contract gives the buyer an interest in the property that is called equitable title, or *ownership in equity*. If the seller defaults and the buyer can show good faith performance, the buyer can sue for specific performance, that is, to compel the seller to transfer legal title upon payment of the contract price.

Earnest money escrow

The buyer's earnest money deposit fulfills the consideration requirements for a valid sale contract. In addition, it provides potential compensation for damages to the seller if the buyer fails to perform. The amount of the deposit varies according to local custom. It should be noted that the earnest money deposit is not the only form of consideration that satisfies the requirement.

The sale contract provides the *escrow instructions* for handling and disbursing escrow funds. The earnest money is placed in a third party trust account or escrow. A licensed escrow agent employed by a title company, financial institution, or brokerage company usually manages the escrow. An individual broker may also serve as the escrow agent.

The escrow holder acts as an impartial fiduciary for buyer and seller. If the buyer performs under the sale contract, the deposit is applied to the purchase price.

Strict rules govern the handling of earnest money deposits, particularly if a broker is the escrow agent. For example, state laws direct the broker when to deposit the funds, how to account for them, and how to keep them separate from the broker's own funds.

Contract contingencies

A sale contract often contains contingencies. A contingency is a condition that must be met before the contract is enforceable.

The most common contingency concerns financing. A buyer makes an offer contingent upon securing financing for the property under certain terms on or before a certain date. If unable to secure the specified loan commitment by the deadline, the buyer may cancel the contract and recover the deposit. An appropriate and timely loan commitment eliminates the contingency, and the buyer must proceed with the purchase.

It is possible for both buyers and sellers to abuse contingencies in order to leave themselves a convenient way to cancel without defaulting. To avoid problems, the statement of a contingency should:

> ▶ be explicit and clear
> ▶ have an expiration date
> ▶ expressly require diligence in the effort to fulfill the requirement

A contingency that is too broad, vague, or excessive in duration may invalidate the entire contract on the grounds of insufficiency of mutual agreement.

Default

A sale contract is bilateral, since both parties promise to perform. As a result, either party may default by failing to perform. Note that a party's failure to meet a contingency does not constitute default, but rather entitles the parties to cancel the contract.

Buyer default. If a buyer fails to perform under the terms of a sale contract, the breach entitles the seller to legal recourse for damages. In most cases, the contract itself stipulates the seller's remedies. The usual remedy is forfeiture of the buyer's deposit as **liquidated damages**, provided the deposit is not grossly in excess of the seller's actual damages. It is also customary to provide for the seller and broker to share the liquidated damages. The broker may not, however, receive liquidated damages in excess of what the commission would have been on the full listing price.

If the contract does not provide for liquidated damages, the seller may sue for damages, cancellation, or specific performance.

Seller default. If a seller defaults, the buyer may sue for specific performance, damages, or cancellation.

SALE CONTRACT PROVISIONS

Sale contracts can vary significantly in length and thoroughness. They also vary according to the type of sale transaction they describe. Some of the varieties are:

> ▶ Residential Contract of Sale
> ▶ Commercial Contract of Sale
> ▶ Foreclosure Contract of Sale
> ▶ Contract of Sale for New Construction
> ▶ Contract of Sale for Land
> ▶ Exchange Agreement

As the most common sale transaction is a residential sale, a Residential Contract of Sale is the type with which a licensee should first become familiar.

Primary provisions

A typical residential sale contract contains provisions of the following kind.

Parties, consideration, and property. One or more clauses will identify the parties, the property, and the basic consideration, which is the sale of the property in return for a purchase price.

There must be at least two parties to a sale contract: one cannot convey property to oneself. All parties must be identified, be of legal age, and have the capacity to contract.

The property clause also identifies fixtures and personal property included in the sale. Unless expressly excluded, items commonly construed as fixtures are *included* in the sale. Similarly, items commonly considered personal property are *not included* unless expressly included.

Legal description. A legal description must be sufficient for a competent surveyor to identify the property.

Price and terms. A clause states the final price and details how the purchase will occur. Of particular interest to the seller is the buyer's down payment, since the greater the buyer's equity, the more likely the buyer will be able to secure financing. In addition, a large deposit represents a buyer's commitment to complete the sale.

If seller financing is involved, the sale contract sets forth the terms of the arrangement: the amount and type of loan, the rate and term, and how the loan will be paid off.

It is important for all parties to verify that the buyer's earnest money deposit, down payment, loan proceeds, and other promised funds together equal the purchase price stated in the contract.

Loan approval. A financing contingency clause states under what conditions the buyer can cancel the contract without default and receive a refund of the earnest money. If the buyer cannot secure the stated financing by the deadline, the parties may agree to extend the contingency by signing next to the changed dates.

Earnest money deposit. A clause specifies how the buyer will pay the earnest money. It may allow the buyer to pay it in installments. Such an option enables a buyer to hold on to the property briefly while obtaining the additional deposit funds. For example, a buyer who wants to buy a house makes an initial deposit of $200, to be followed in twenty-four hours with an additional $2,000. The sale contract includes the seller's acknowledgment of receipt of the deposit.

Escrow. An escrow clause provides for the custody and disbursement of the earnest money deposit, and releases the escrow agent from certain liabilities in the performance of escrow duties.

Closing and possession dates. The contract states when title will transfer, as well as when the buyer will take physical possession. Customarily, possession occurs on the date when the deed is recorded, unless the buyer has agreed to other arrangements.

The closing clause generally describes what must take place at closing to avoid default. A seller must provide clear and marketable title. A buyer must produce purchase funds. Failure to complete any pre-closing requirements stated in the sale contract is default and grounds for the aggrieved party to seek recourse.

Conveyed interest; type of deed. One or more provisions will state what type of deed the seller will use to convey the property, and what conditions the deed will be subject to. Among common "subject to" conditions are easements, association memberships, encumbrances, mortgages, liens, and special assessments. Typically, the seller conveys a fee simple interest by means of a general warranty deed.

Title evidence. The seller covenants to produce the best possible evidence of property ownership. This is commonly in the form of title insurance.

Closing costs. The contract identifies which closing costs each party will pay. Customarily, the seller pays title and property-related costs, and the buyer pays financing-related costs. Annual costs such as taxes and insurance are prorated between the parties. Note that who pays any particular closing cost is an item for negotiation.

Damage and destruction. A clause stipulates the obligations of the parties in case the property is damaged or destroyed. The parties may negotiate alternatives, including seller's obligation to repair, buyer's obligation to buy if repairs are made, and the option for either party to cancel.

Default. A default clause identifies remedies for default. Generally, a buyer may sue for damages, specific performance, or cancellation. A seller may do likewise or claim the earnest money as liquidated damages.

Broker's representation and commission. The broker discloses the applicable agency relationships in the transaction and names the party who must pay the brokerage commission.

Seller's representations. The seller warrants that there will be no liens on the property that cannot be settled and extinguished at closing. In addition, the seller warrants that all representations are true, and if found otherwise, the buyer may cancel the contract and reclaim the deposit.

Inspections. The parties agree to inspections and remedial action based on findings.

Owner's association disclosure. The seller discloses existence of an association and the obligations it imposes.

Environmental hazards. The seller notifies the buyer that there may be hazards that could affect the use and value of the property.

Condominium assessments. Seller discloses assessments the owner must pay.

Time is of the essence. The parties agree that they can amend dates and deadlines only if they both give written approval.

C.L.U.E. Report. CLUE (Comprehensive Loss Underwriting Exchange) is a claims history database used by insurance companies in underwriting or rating insurance policies. A CLUE Home Seller's Disclosure Report shows a five-year insurance loss history for a specific property.

Addenda. Addenda to the sale contract become binding components of the overall agreement. The most common addendum is the seller's property condition disclosure. Examples of other addenda are:

agency disclosure	asbestos / hazardous materials
liquidated damages	radon disclosure
flood plain disclosure	tenant's lease

OPTION-TO-BUY CONTRACT

An option-to-buy is an enforceable contract in which a potential seller, the **optionor**, grants a potential buyer, the **optionee**, the right to purchase a property before a stated time for a stated price and terms. In exchange for the right of option, the optionee pays the optionor valuable consideration.

For example, a buyer wants to purchase a property for $150,000, but needs to sell a boat to raise the down payment. The boat will take two or three months to sell. To accommodate the buyer, the seller offers the buyer an option to purchase the property at any time before midnight on the day that is ninety days from the date of signing the option. The buyer pays the seller $1,000 for the option. If buyer exercises the option, the seller will apply the $1,000 toward the earnest money deposit and subsequent down payment. If the optionee lets the option expire, the seller keeps the $1,000. Both parties agree to the arrangement by completing a sale contract as an addendum to the option, then executing the option agreement itself.

Unilateral agreement. An option-to-buy places the optionee *under no obligation* to purchase the property. However, the seller must perform under the terms of the contract if the buyer exercises the option. An option is thus a *unilateral* agreement. Exercise of the option creates a bilateral sale contract where both parties are bound to perform. An unused option terminates at the expiration date.

Lease options-to-buy. An optionee can use an option to prevent the sale of a property to another party while seeking to raise funds for the purchase. A renter with a **lease option-to-buy** can accumulate down payment funds while paying rent to the landlord. For example, an owner may lease a condominium to a tenant with an option to buy. If the tenant takes the option, the landlord agrees to apply $100 of the monthly rent paid prior to the option date toward the purchase price. The tenant pays the landlord the nominal sum of $200 for the option.

Options can also facilitate commercial property acquisition. The option period gives a buyer time to investigate zoning, space planning, building permits, environmental impacts, and other feasibility issues prior to the purchase without losing the property to another party in the meantime.

Contract requirements

To be valid and enforceable, an option-to-buy must:

- include actual, non-refundable consideration

  The option must require the optionee to pay a specific consideration *that is separate from the purchase price*. The consideration cannot be refunded if the option is not exercised. If the option is exercised, the consideration may be applied to the purchase price. If the option is a lease option, portions of the rent may qualify as separate consideration.

- include price and terms of the sale

  The price and terms of the potential transaction must be clearly expressed and cannot change over the option period. It is customary practice for the parties to complete and attach a sale contract to the option as satisfaction of this requirement.

- have an expiration date

  The option must automatically expire at the end of a specific period.

- be in writing

  Since a potential transfer of real estate is involved, most state statutes of fraud require an option to be in writing.

- include a legal description

- meet general contract validity requirements

  The basics include competent parties, the optionor's promise to perform, and the optionor's signature. Note that it is not necessary for the optionee to sign the option.

Legal aspects

Equitable interest. The optionee enjoys an equitable interest in the property because the option creates the right to obtain legal title. However, the option does not in itself convey an interest in real property, only a right to do something governed by contract law.

Recording. An option should be recorded, because the equitable interest it creates can affect the marketability of title.

Assignment. An option-to-buy is assignable unless the contract expressly prohibits assignment.

A contract for deed is also called a *land contract*, an *installment sale*, a *conditional sales contract,* and an *agreement for deed*. It is a bilateral agreement between a seller, the **vendor,** and a buyer, the **vendee**, in which the vendor defers receipt of some or all of the purchase price of a property over a specified period of time. During the period, the *vendor retains legal title* and the vendee acquires equitable title. The vendee takes possession of the property, makes stipulated payments of principal and interest to the vendor, and otherwise fulfills obligations as the contract requires. At the end of the period, the buyer pays the vendor the full purchase price and the vendor deeds legal title to the vendee.

Like an option, a contract for deed offers a means for a marginally qualified buyer to acquire property. In essence, the seller acts as lender, allowing the buyer to take possession and pay off the purchase price over time. A buyer may thus avoid conventional down payment and income requirements imposed by institutional lenders. During the contract period, the buyer can work to raise the necessary cash to complete the purchase or to qualify for a conventional mortgage.

A contract for deed serves two primary purposes for a seller. First, it facilitates a sale that might otherwise be impossible. Second, it may give the seller certain tax benefits. Since the seller is not liable for capital gains tax until the purchase price is received, the installment sale lowers the seller's tax liability in the year of the sale.

Interests and rights

Vendor's rights and obligations. During the contract period, the seller may:

- mortgage the property
- sell or assign whatever interests he or she owns in the property to another party
- incur judgment liens against the property

The vendor, however, is bound to the obligations imposed by the contract for deed. In particular, the vendor may not breach the obligation to convey legal title to the vendee upon receipt of the total purchase price. In addition, the vendor remains liable for underlying mortgage loans.

Vendee's rights and obligations. During the contract period, the buyer may occupy, use, enjoy, and profit from the property, subject to the provisions of the written agreement. The vendee must make periodic payments of principal and interest and maintain the property. In addition, a vendee may have to pay property taxes and hazard insurance.

Legal form

Like other conveyance contracts, a contract for deed instrument identifies:

- the principal parties
- the property's legal description
- consideration: specifically what the parties promise to do
- the terms of the sale
- obligations for property maintenance

>   ▶   default and remedies
>   ▶   signatures and acknowledgment

The contract specifies the vendee's payments, payment deadlines, when the balance of the purchase price is due, and how the property may be used.

Default and recourse   **Seller default.** If the seller defaults, such as by failing to deliver the deed, the buyer may sue for specific performance, or for cancellation of the agreement and damages.

Buyer default. States differ in the remedies they prescribe for the seller in case of buyer default. Some states consider the default a breach of contract that may be remedied by cancellation, retention of monies received, and eviction. Others provide foreclosure proceedings as a remedy.

Usage guidelines   Many areas have no standardized contract for deed or any form sanctioned by associations and agencies. Therefore, this kind of conveyance presents certain pitfalls for buyer and seller.

In some states, a breach of the contract for deed is remedied under *local contract law* rather than foreclosure law. The buyer may not have the protections of a redemption period or other buyer-protection laws which accompany formal foreclosure proceedings. The vendor might sue the vendee for breach of contract for the slightest infraction of the contract terms.

A second danger for the vendee is that the vendor has the power and the right to encumber the property in ways that may not be desirable for the buyer. For example, the seller could place a home equity loan on the property, then fail to make periodic payments. The bank could then foreclose on the vendor, thus jeopardizing the vendee's eventual purchase.

For the seller, the principal danger is that the buyer acquires possession in exchange for a minimal down payment. A buyer might damage or even vacate the property, leaving the seller to make repairs and retake possession. Further, since the contract is recorded, the seller must also bear the time and expense of clearing the title.

To minimize risk, principal parties in a contract for deed should observe the following guidelines:

>   ▶   use an attorney to draft the agreement
>   ▶   adopt the standard forms, if available
>   ▶   become familiar with how the contract will be enforced
>   ▶   utilize professional escrow and title services
>   ▶   record the transaction properly
>   ▶   be prepared for the possible effect on existing financing

Check Your Understanding Quiz:

Chapter 2: Overview of Conveyance Contracts

Carefully read each question and provide your best answer based on what you learned in this module. Then check your answers against the Answer Key which immediately follows the quiz questions.

1. Upon entering a contract to purchase real property the

   a. buyer obtains equitable title.
   b. seller obtains equitable title.
   c. buyer obtains legal title.
   d. seller obtains legal title.

2. An option-to-purchase contract is a(n)

   a. bilateral contract.
   b. unilateral contract.
   c. reciprocal contract.
   d. installment sales contract.

3. Which of the following is NOT one of the three stages in the conventional transfer of real property?

   a. Negotiating-to-contracting period
   b. Preclosing
   c. Closing
   d. Analysis stage

4. In an executory contract, the

   a. parties are yet to perform their obligations.
   b. parties have performed all their obligations.
   c. contract is performed by an executor.
   d. the contract is performed by a trustee.

5. Upon entering an option agreement for the purchase of real property, the buyer obtains

   a. an extinguishable interest.
   b. a reversion.
   c. legal title.
   d. equitable title.

6. The failure of a contract contingency to be fulfilled

   a. triggers a default by the party responsible for the contingency to occur.
   b. nullifies the contract.
   c. relieves a party of the obligation of further performance.
   d. creates grounds for a reduced purchase price.

7. A contract for the purchase of real property is a(n)

   a. unilateral contract.
   b. bilateral contract.
   c. voidable contract.
   d. a void contract.

8. If a buyer defaults on a contract for the purchase of real property, a common remedy for the seller is

   a. specific performance
   b. liquidated damages.
   c. an injunction.
   d. disciplinary action against the buyer's licensee.

9. In a contract for deed, before the final payment is made, the buyer has

   a. equitable title with a right to possession.
   b. equitable title but no right of possession.
   c. legal title with the right of possession.
   d. legal title without the right of possession.

10. Which of the following is another name for a contract for deed?

   a. Land option.
   b. Installment sale contract.
   c. Contract for equitable title.
   d. Contract for sale.

Answer Key:

Chapter 2: Overview of Conveyance Contracts

1. a. buyer obtains equitable title.

2. b. unilateral contract.

3. d. Analysis stage

4. a. parties are yet to perform their obligations.

5. d. equitable title.

6. c. relieves a party of the obligation of further performance.

7. b. bilateral contract.

8. b. liquidated damages.

9. a. equitable title with a right to possession.

10. b. installment sales contract.

Chapter 3:
Nevada Conveyance and
Management Contracts

Standard forms and mandated forms

In the practice of real estate, licensees use many types of forms and contracts. Some of these forms are created and their use mandated by the Nevada Real Estate Division. Others are simply standard forms available through boards of REALTORS® and local real estate associations for the licensee's use. These forms have been written by attorneys for the particular organizations.

Mandated forms include disclosures, such as a Consent to Act, Authority to Negotiate Directly with Seller, and so on. Standard, but not mandated forms include residential purchase offers, brokerage agreements, leases, and so forth.

Most standard forms can be found online on various real estate organization websites. Mandated forms can be found online at the Division's website http://red.nv.gov/Content/Forms/Main/.

Practicing law without a license. Sometimes a situation may arise where there is no preprinted standard form that applies. In these cases, the licensee or broker may be tempted to prepare the document him or herself. However, while Nevada laws are not clear on a broker's authority to prepare documents related to a real estate transaction, the laws are clear on prohibiting a broker from practicing law if he or she is not a licensed attorney. The confusion comes from the law's lack of clarity on what activities fall under the practice of law. So, to be safe, it is always better to have an attorney prepare any new documents that may not already be available.

Statute of frauds. While some contracts, such as brokerage agreements, may be oral, others are required to be in writing. For example, purchase agreements must be in writing, as must a lease agreement for more than 1 year. The statute of frauds requires these contracts to be in writing and signed by the involved parties.

Retention of forms. Any document completed by a licensee must be turned over to the broker within 5 days of signing and retained in the broker's files for 5 years.

Nevada's statute of frauds requires that all purchase agreements be in writing. So, while an offer is legal if it is given verbally, if the acceptance is also verbal, no legally binding contract or purchase agreement has been created. To convert a verbal offer and acceptance into a legal and enforceable purchase agreement, the contract must be in writing. It must also show the consideration and be signed by the seller.

Offers. All offers must be presented to the seller unless the seller has signed a waiver. What is a licensee to do if there are multiple offers?

There are no statutes or rules prescribing the order in which multiple offers must be presented to the seller. As long as all offers are presented to the seller as soon as practicable with the terms of the offers, then the licensee is in compliance with the law. The best course of action would be to discuss with the seller when the property is listed how the seller would like multiple offers presented and handled.

To assist licensees, the Division has published specific guidelines for how licensees should handle multiple offers. Those guidelines can be found on the Division's website at http://red.nv.gov/uploadedFiles/rednvgov/Content/Publications/Bulletins/ib01-multipleoffers.pdf.

Among the various ways of handling multiple offers, the seller has the option to

▶ accept one offer and reject all others
▶ negotiate all offers to encourage higher offers
▶ negotiate one offer and reject all others
▶ hold all offers and wait for a new, higher offer

Acceptance. When the seller has decided on one offer to accept, the acceptance should be in writing and delivered to the buyer or the buyer's agent in a reasonable manner – mail, hand delivery, email, or fax. Once the signed acceptance is delivered to the buyer or buyer's agent, a binding purchase agreement exists. All other offerors should be notified that their offers have been rejected and asked to sign the rejection notice.

Purchase agreement. The same form can be used to present an offer and to accept the offer and, thus, create a purchase agreement. A purchase agreement is also known as an offer and acceptance, a contract of sale, a sales contract, or a purchase contract.

Purchase agreements are required to include what general contract law calls the "four Ps" – parties, property, price, and proof (consideration). For the contract to be legal and enforceable, the following requirements must be met:

▶ all signing parties must be at least 18 years old

    ▸ all signing parties must be legally competent, that is, not insane or inebriated (alcohol or drugs) to the point of being devoid of all understanding

    ▸ the contract must be in writing, state the consideration given by the parties to the contract, and be signed; emails meet the "must be in writing" requirement based on the Nevada Electronic Transaction Act.

Consideration. All purchase agreements require consideration, which may be mutual obligations or something of value exchanged between the parties. The mutual obligation occurs when each party has some right or benefit and some responsibility or burden. When mutual obligation is met, the requirement for consideration is met.

Signatures. Because the purchase agreement includes obligations from both the seller and the buyer, they must each accept the obligations by each signing the agreement. Nevada is a community property state, so both spouses in a married couple buying the property must sign the agreement. Both spouses selling the property are not required to sign the agreement but must execute the deed to transfer the title. To avoid complications, licensees should have both selling spouses sign the agreement even though not required by law. Signing may be done by electronic signature.

Copies. Licensees are required to deliver a copy of the purchase agreement to both the buyer and the seller within a reasonable time after signing. The licensee is also required to provide a copy of the agreement to his or her broker within 5 days after signing, and the broker must retain the copy for at least 5 years whether or not the transaction ever closed.

Earnest money. Earnest money is typically included with an offer to support the offer. The earnest money must be deposited into the listing broker's trust account before the end of the next banking day unless the offer or purchase agreement states other provisions. If the offer is accepted, the earnest money becomes part of the buyer's down payment. If the offer is rejected, the earnest money is refunded to the offeror.

RESIDENTIAL LEASES

Lease requirements. Nevada mandates provisions for landlords and tenants within NRS 118A. The law defines a rental agreement as "any oral or written agreement for the use and occupancy of a dwelling unit or premises." A rental agreement, or lease, for one year or less may be oral. An agreement for more than one year must be in writing. Written agreements must be signed by both the landlord and the tenant, and the landlord must provide the tenant with a copy of the lease at the time the agreement is signed.

Written leases must also contain the following:

    ▸ the duration of the agreement

    ▸ the amount of rent and how and when it is to be paid

- ▶ whether children or pets will be occupants
- ▶ services to be included
- ▶ additional fees and their purposes
- ▶ required deposits and how they are to be refunded
- ▶ late charges and dishonored check charges
- ▶ the landlord's inspection rights
- ▶ a list of persons who will occupy the unit
- ▶ who will pay utility charges
- ▶ a signed inventory and condition of the premises prior to occupancy
- ▶ information on how the tenant may report problems to the appropriate authorities
- ▶ the tenant's right to display the U.S. flag
- ▶ the name, address, and telephone number of the landlord

Security deposit. The security deposit may not exceed three months' rent and is to be allocated for unpaid rent, damage repairs, and cleaning. When the tenancy terminates by either party, the landlord may use the security deposit for any of those expenses and then must provide the tenant with an itemized accounting of how the deposit funds were spent. Any funds left are to be returned to the tenant within 30 days after the tenancy termination, or the landlord is liable for damages.

Landlord duties. During the tenancy, the landlord is responsible for maintaining the unit in a habitable condition by assuring it contains

- ▶ effective waterproofing and weather protection
- ▶ working plumbing facilities
- ▶ a water supply that is connected to a sewage disposal system pursuant to applicable law
- ▶ adequate heating and electrical facilities
- ▶ adequate garbage receptacles and removal
- ▶ clean and sanitary building, grounds, and appurtenances
- ▶ floors, walls, ceilings, stairways, & railings in good repair
- ▶ ventilating, air-conditioning, and other appliances in good repair

Tenant responsibilities. The tenant has the responsibility to keep the premises clean and free of destruction, to comply with the terms of the lease, and to conduct him or herself in a manner that does not create a nuisance.

Landlord rights. The landlord may evict the tenant for the following reasons and with the following notice:

- ▶ termination of lease – 5 days
- ▶ nonpayment of rent – 5 days

- ▸ breach of lease – 5 days
- ▸ creating a nuisance – 3 days
- ▸ no cause for week-to-week (7 days) or month-to-month (30 days)

PROPERTY MANAGEMENT AGREEMENTS

Permit. Real estate licensees who wish to engage in property management must obtain a property management permit. A broker who wants to add property management to the services he or she provides may designate a broker-salesperson to obtain the permit and perform the property management.

Agreement requirements. Property managers must have written property management agreements with each client. Remember that a property management agreement is not a brokerage agreement. The management agreement is a written employment contract between the broker and the client wherein the broker agrees to accept compensation to manage the client's property.

The property management agreement must be in writing and include the term of employment. Unlike brokerage agreements, the property management agreement may have an automatic renewal provision as long as the provision includes how the renewal will take place and the length of the renewal period.

The agreement must include how much the broker will be paid and if the payment will be a flat fee, a percentage of the rents, or something else. The agreement must also include how the manager is to handle the rents and deposits collected and whether or not the manager may initiate evictions. Cancellation or termination of the agreement (with or without cause) must also be included.

Agreement components

The management agreement establishes an agency agreement between manager and owner as well as specifying such essentials as the manager's scope of authority, responsibilities, objectives, compensation, and the term of the agreement.

Property managers are usually considered to be general agents empowered to perform some or all of the ongoing tasks and duties of operating the property, including the authority to enter into contracts. The agency relationship creates the fiduciary duties of obedience, care, loyalty, accounting, and disclosure. The contractual relationship ensures that the manager will strive to realize the highest return for the owner consistent with the owner's objectives and instructions.

The agreement should be in writing and include at least the basics of any real estate contract, as follows.

- ▸ **Names of the parties**--owner, landlord, manager, tenant or other party to be bound by the contract

- **Property description**--street address, unit number and location, square footage, and other information that specifies the leased premises

- **Term**--time period (months, years) covered by the contract; termination conditions and provisions

- **Owner's purpose**--maximize net income, maximize asset value, maximize return, minimize expenditure, maintain property quality, etc.; long-term goals for the property

- **Owner's responsibilities**--management fees, plus any management expenses such as payroll, advertising and insurance that the manager will not be expected to pay

- **Manager's authority**--the **scope** of powers being conveyed to the manager: hiring and staffing, setting rents, contracting with vendors, ordering repairs, limits on expenditures without seeking owner permission

- **Manager's responsibilities**--specification of duties, such as marketing, leasing, maintenance, budgeting, reporting, collecting and handling rents; the manager should be included as an additional insured on the liability policy for the property

- **Budget**--amounts, or percentages of revenues, allotted for operations, taxes, insurance, capital expenditures, etc.

- **Allocation of costs**--who is to pay certain expenses, that is, which will be treated as expenses of the manager vs. which will be paid directly by the owner

- **Reporting**--how often and what kind of reports are to be made

- **Compensation**--the management fee or other means of compensation to the manager; there may be a flat fee based on square footage, a rental commission based on a percentage of annual rent, a combination of these, or some other arrangement; in compliance with anti-trust laws, management fees are not standardized but must be negotiated by agent and principal

- **Equal opportunity statement**--the HUD statement or equivalent concerning availability to all persons and classes protected by law, incorporated into the agreement in the case of a residential property

Manager's duties. Depending on the degree of authority granted by the agreement, the manager may have the right to hire and fire, enter into contracts, and perform routine management tasks without interference from the owner. The manager has the duties described earlier: to maintain financial records and make reports; to budget; to find, retain, and collect from tenants; to maintain and secure the property; to meet the owner's objectives. The manager's liabilities include the consequences of mishandling trust funds, violating fiduciary responsibilities, and violating fair housing laws, credit laws, and employment laws.

Trust accounts. Property managers are required to maintain two trust accounts – one for security deposits and one for rents and rental operations.

Informational Bulletin #012 regarding property management can be found at http://red.nv.gov/uploadedFiles/rednvgov/Content/Publications/Bulletins/IB12 PropertyManagement.pdf and includes information on activities a property manager may perform and what actions can be taken if an unlicensed and unpermitted person performs activities that require a license and permit.

Sample Management Agreement

MANAGEMENT AGREEMENT

Agreement made_____*[date]*, between_____, a corporation organized under the laws of the State of _____, having its principal office at_____*[address]*,_____*[city]*,_____*[state]*, here referred to as owner, and_____, a corporation organized under the laws of the State of_____, having its principal office at a*ddress]*,_____*[city]*,_____*[state]*, here referred to as agent.

RECITALS

1. Owner holds title to the following-described real property:_____*[insert legal or other appropriate description]*, here referred to as the property.
2. Agent is experienced in the business of operating and managing real estate similar to the above-described property.
3. Owner desires to engage the services of agent to manage and operate the property, and agent desires to provide such services on the following terms and conditions.

In consideration of the mutual covenants contained herein, the parties agree:

EMPLOYMENT OF AGENT. Agent shall act as the exclusive agent of owner to manage, operate, and maintain the property.

BEST EFFORTS OF AGENT. On assuming the management and operation of the property, agent shall thoroughly inspect the property and submit a written report to owner concerning the present efficiency under which the property is being managed and operated, and recommended changes, if necessary.

LEASING OF PROPERTY. Agent shall make reasonable efforts to lease available space of the property, and shall be responsible for all negotiations with prospective tenants. Agent shall also have the right to execute and enter into, on behalf of owner, month-to-month tenancies of units of the property.

ADVERTISING AND PROMOTION. Agent shall advertise vacancies by all reasonable and proper means; provided, agent shall not incur expenses for advertising in excess of____Dollars ($_____) during any calendar quarter without the prior written consent of owner.

MAINTENANCE, REPAIRS, AND OPERATIONS. Agent shall use its best efforts to insure that the property is maintained in an attractive condition and in a good state of repair. Expenditures for repairs, alterations, decorations or furnishings in excess of_____Dollars ($_____) shall not be made without prior written consent of owner.

EMPLOYEES. Agent shall employ, discharge, and supervise all on-site employees or contractors required for the efficient operation and maintenance of the property. All on-site personnel, except independent contractors and employees of independent contractors, shall be the employees of agent.

INSURANCE. Agent shall obtain the following insurance at the expense of owner, and such insurance shall be maintained in force during the full term of this agreement:

1. Comprehensive public liability property insurance of _____Dollars ($___) single limit for bodily injury, death, and property damage;

2. Comprehensive automobile insurance of _____ Dollars ($_____) single limit for bodily injury, death, and property damage;

3. Fire and extended coverage hazard insurance in an amount equal to the full replacement cost of the structure and other improvements situated on the property; and

4. A fidelity bond in the amount of_____ Dollars ($_____) on each employee who handles cash, and workers' compensation and employer liability insurance to cover the agents and employees of both employer and agent.

COLLECTION OF INCOME. Agent shall use its best efforts to collect promptly all rents and other income issuing from the property when such amounts become due. It is understood that agent does not guarantee the collection of rents.

BANK ACCOUNTS. Agent shall deposit (either directly or in a depositary bank for transmittal) all revenues from the property into the general property management trust fund of agent, here referred to as the trust account. From the revenues deposited in the trust account, agent shall pay all items with respect to the property for which payment is provided in this agreement, including the compensation of agent and deposits to the reserve accounts as provided for. Agent shall remit any balance of monthly revenues to owner concurrently with the delivery of the monthly report.

RESERVE ACCOUNT. Agent shall establish a reserve account for the following items: taxes, assessments, debt service, insurance premiums, repairs (other than normal maintenance), replacement of personal property, and refundable deposits.

RECORDS AND REPORTS. Agent shall furnish owner, no later than the end of the next succeeding month, a detailed statement of all revenues and expenditures for each preceding month. Within   days after the end of each calendar year, agent shall prepare and deliver to owner a detailed statement of revenues received and expenditures incurred and paid during the calendar year that result from operations of the property.

COMPENSATION OF AGENT. Agent shall receive a management fee equal to __ percent (__ %) of the

gross receipts collected from the operation of the property. Any management fee due agent hereunder shall be paid to agent within _____days after the end of each month.

TERMINATION AND RENEWAL. This agreement shall be for a term commencing on_____[date], and ending on _____[date].

MODIFICATION. This agreement may not be modified unless such modification is in writing and signed by both parties to this agreement.

IN WITNESS WHEREOF, the parties have executed this agreement at [designate place of execution] the

day and year first above written.

Check Your Understanding Quiz:

Chapter 3: Nevada Conveyance and Management Contracts

Carefully read each question and provide your best answer based on what you learned in this module. Then check your answers against the Answer Key which immediately follows the quiz questions.

1. Which of the following best characterizes Nevada's legal stance on licensees completing sales contracts?

    a. Brokers cannot complete any conveyance contract whatsoever.
    b. Broker's may advise clients as to how to complete the contract.
    c. Brokers may complete sales contracts without a law license.
    d. The broker's authority to complete contracts is unclear.

2. A licensee completes a transaction document for a given client. How much time does this licensee have to turn the form over to the broker?

    a. one business day.
    b. within 5 days of signing.
    c. one month.
    d. as soon as is practicable.

3. A seller receives multiple offers on his property. In that context, which of the following is true?

    a. The first full-price offer must be submitted immediately to the seller.
    b. The seller must accept or reject the offers in the order they were received.
    c. The seller has the option to hold all offers and wait for a better offer.
    d. Multiple offers are not valid in Nevada.

4. At what specific point in time does an offer from a buyer to a seller become a binding sale contract?

    a. When the seller notifies his/her agent that she accepts the offer.
    b. When the seller receives an offer that is subsequently accepted in a reasonable amount of time.
    c. When the acceptance is delivered to the buyer or buyer's agent.
    d. When the buyer notifies the seller that he or she has received the seller's acceptance of the offer.

5. Purchase agreements are required to include what general contract law calls the "four Ps". Which of the following is NOT one of the Ps?

    a. Parties
    b. Property
    c. Price
    d. Performance

6. A security deposit for a residential, rental unit, may not legally exceed

   a. 9 months' rent.
   b. 6 months' rent.
   c. 3 months' rent.
   d. 1 months' rent.

7. In a residential, rental unit, who is legally responsible for maintaining the unit in a habitable condition?

   a. The landlord
   b. The tenant
   c. The property manager
   d. The city or county

8. Real estate licensees wishing to practice property management in Nevada

   a. must be a broker managing a brokerage firm.
   b. must obtain a property management license.
   c. must obtain a property management permit.
   d. need only maintain an active real estate license.

9. Which of the following is required by law to be in writing?

   a. Open listing agreement
   b. Rental agreement with a 6-month term
   c. Open buyer representation agreement
   d. Property management agreement

Answer Key:

Chapter 3: Nevada Conveyance and Management Contracts

1. d. The broker's authority to complete contracts is unclear.

2. b. within 5 days of signing.

3. c. The seller has the option to hold all offers and wait for a better offer.

4. c. When the acceptance is delivered to the buyer or buyer's agent.

5. d. Performance

6. c. 3 months' rent.

7. a. The landlord

8. c. must obtain a property management permit.

9. d. Property management agreement

SECTION ONE WORKSHOP – CONVEYANCE AND MANAGEMENT CONTRACTS

(Chapters 1-3)

I. Progress Checkpoints

Carefully read each question then provide your best answer based on what you learned in the Contracts Section. Then check your answers against the Answer Key which immediately follows the questions.

1. The text identifies 5 criteria that must be met to have a valid contract. List two of them:

    1. _____

    2. _____

5. List two contracts that the statute of frauds requires to be in writing.

    1. _____

    2. _____

3. Any document completed by a Nevada licensee must be turned over to the broker within ____ days of signing and retained in the broker's files for ____ years.

4. What happens to a buyer's earnest money deposit if the buyer's offer is not accepted?

    _____

5. A security deposit for the rental of residential unit, in Nevada, must not exceed _____.

6. List at least three provisions that must be included in a written residential lease.

    1. _____

    2. _____

    3. _____

7. Describe the two trust accounts that must be maintained by a Nevada property manager.

    1. _____

    2. _____

I. Progress Checkpoints: Answer Key

1. The text identifies 5 criteria that must be met to have a valid contract List two of them:
   The 5 criteria are:

   1. competent parties

   2. mutual consent

   3. valuable consideration

   4. legal purpose

   5. voluntary act of good faith

2. List two contracts that the statute of frauds requires to be in writing.

   1. **A contract for the purchase or sale of real property.**

   2. **A lease with a term in excess of one year.**

3. Any document completed by a Nevada licensee must be turned over to the broker within <u>5 calendar days</u> of signing and retained in the broker's files for <u>5 years</u>.

4. What happens to a buyer's earnest money deposit if the buyer's offer is not accepted?

   The earnest money is returned to the buyer.

5. A security deposit for the rental of residential unit, Nevada, must not exceed **3 months**.

6. List at least three provisions that must be included in a written residential lease.

   1. **The duration of the agreement**

   2. **The amount of rent and how and when it is to be paid**

   3. **Whether occupants will include children or pets**

Other provisions include

- services to be included
- additional fees and their purposes
- required deposits and how they are to be refunded
- late charges and dishonored check charges
- the landlord's inspection rights

- a list of persons who will occupy the unit
- who will pay utility charges
- a signed inventory and condition of the premises prior to occupancy
- information on how the tenant may report problems to the appropriate authorities
- the tenant's right to display the U.S. flag
- the name, address, and telephone number of the landlord

7. Describe the two trust accounts that must be maintained by a Nevada property manager.

1. **A trust account for security deposits**

2. **A trust account for rents and rental operations**

II. Applied Practices Exercises

Carefully read each set of instructions then provide your best answer based on what you learned in the Contracts units. Then check your answers against the de-brier answers which immediately follow the questions.

1. **Exercise 1: Liquidated Damages.**

   Exercise 1: Synopsis. In many real estate purchase contracts, the parties can choose to include a liquidated damages clause which specifies the amount of money that the seller will recover in the event of a buyer defaults. It is common to designate the earnest money deposit is the liquidated amount. A liquidated damages clause provides a benefit and a detriment to the buyer and the seller. Identify and explain the benefits and detriments of a liquidated damages clause by completing the table below.

   ### SAMPLE LIQUIDATED DAMAGES CLAUSE

   BUYER DEFAULT BUYER must initial only one of the following.
   If BUYER defaults in the performance of this Agreement, SELLER shall have the right to:
   A. [_____/_____] (BUYER Initials) Liquidated Damages: SELLER shall have the right to retain, as their sole legal recourse, the EMD. BUYER and SELLER hereby acknowledge SELLER's actual damages would be difficult to measure and that the EMD is a fair and reasonable estimate of such damages.
   OR
   B. [_____/_____] (BUYER Initials) Actual Damages: SELLER shall have the right to recover from BUYER all of SELLER's actual damages that SELLER may suffer as a result of BUYER's default, and to pursue any and all remedies available at law or in equity.

Exercise 1: Instructions: Complete the following benefit/detriment table as a summary of the advantages and disadvantages of the provisions of the liquidated damages clause and its alternative actions. Refer to the sample clause provided and use your experience and knowledge to present your entries.

LIQUIDATED DAMAGES CLAUSE		
	Benefit	Detriment
Buyer		
Seller		

Exercise 1: De-brief answers / solutions / recommendations

LIQUIDATED DAMAGES CLAUSE		
	Benefit	**Detriment**
Buyer	Buyer will know exactly how much it will cost to get out of the contract without providing a reason.	The liquidated amount might be much greater than any actual damages sustained by the seller.
Seller	If the buyer breaches (defaults) the seller does not have to prove any damages. The seller is entitled to the liquidated amount.	The liquidated amount might be much less than the actual damages sustained by the seller.

Exercise 2: Matching Contract Classifications

Exercise 2 Instructions: Match the contract type in the left column with its classification in the right column. (unilateral v bilateral; executed v executory; express v implied). Note that some classifications match more than one contract type. When you have completed your matching, review the answers provided.

CONTRACT	CLASSIFICATION
Option	Unilateral
Neither party has performed	Bilateral
Both parties have performed	Executed
Reward contract	Executory
Purchase agreement	Express
Created by conduct	Implied
Created without a writing	
Rental agreement	
Brokerage agreement	

Exercise 2: Matching solutions

Option:	**Unilateral**
Neither party has performed:	**Executory**
Both parties have performed:	**Executed**
Purchase agreement:	**Bilateral**
Created by conduct:	**Implied**
Created without a writing:	**Oral**
Rental Agreement:	**Bilateral**
Brokerage Agreement:	**Bilateral**

Exercise 3: Contracts formation case study:

Exercise 3 Synopsis: In this exercise, Bob and Sally are negotiating for the sale of Sally's house to Bob. In the scenario, numerous stages in negotiations are presented. The challenge is to assess each event, the legal effect, and whether or not such an action constitutes the formation of a contract.

Exercise 3: Instructions: A summary of Bob and Sally's negotiations is provided in the table below. All communications took place in writing. Analyze what took place each day and state the legal effect of what action transpired.

DAY 1	Bob offered to buy Sally's house for $450,000. All other required terms and conditions were included in the offer. **Action summary / legal effect**:
DAY 2	Sally receives an offer from Pete to buy her house for $460,000. Offer to remain open for 3 days. **Action summary/ legal effect**:
DAY 3	Sally sends an email to Bob stating, "Let's make it $465,000 and we have a deal." **Action summary/ legal effect**:
DAY 3	Bob sends a reply to Sally's email stating, "No Thanks". **Action summary/ legal effect**:
DAY 4	Pete sends an email to Sally revoking his offer. **Action summary/ legal effect**:
DAY 4	Sally sends an email to Pete reminding him that his offer is open until Day 5 and accepts his offer for $460,000. **Action summary/ legal effect**:
DAY 4	Sally also received and accepted an offer from Mayra. **Action summary/ legal effect**:

DAY 4	To make sure she had a contract with someone Sally sent an email to Bob saying, "OK, I will accept your original offer for $450,000. **Action summary/ legal effect**: _____ _____
DAY 5	Sally receives a letter from an attorney with a certified court order showing that Mayra had been judicially declared incompetent. **Action summary/ legal effect**: _____ _____

Exercise 3: De-brief answers / solutions / recommendations

Sally does not have a valid contract with anyone to sell her house.	
DAY 1	Bob offered to buy Sally's house for $450,000. All other required terms and conditions were included in the offer. **Bob makes a valid offer to buy Sally's house for $450,000.**
DAY 2	Sally receives an offer from Pete to buy her house for $460,000. All other required terms and conditions were included in the offer. Offer to remain open for 3 days. **Pete makes an offer to buy Sally's house for $460,000. Offer to remain open for 3 days, but there is no consideration for that promise.**
DAY 3	Sally sends an email to Bob stating, "Let's make it $465,000 and we have a deal." **Sally makes a counteroffer to Bob to sell her house for $465,000. This terminates Bob's offer.**
DAY 3	Bob sends a reply to Sally's email stating, "No Thanks". **Bob rejects Sally's counteroffer. This terminates Sally's counteroffer. There is no offer/counteroffer between Bob and Sally on the table.**
DAY 4	Pete sends an email to Sally revoking his offer. **Pete revokes his offer before the 3-day deadline. There is no other legal effect because there is no consideration to leave the offer open.**
DAY 4	Sally sends an email to Pete reminding him that his offer is open until Day 5 and accepts his offer for $460,000. **Sally purports to accept Pete's offer but her "acceptance" is ineffective because Pete revoked the offer before it was accepted.**
DAY 4	Sally also received and accepted an offer from Mayra. **Sally accepts an offer from Mayra.**
DAY 4	To make sure she had a contract with someone Sally sent an email to Bob saying, "OK, I will accept your original offer for $450,000." **Sally purports to accept Bob's original offer, but that offer has been terminated.**
DAY 5	Sally receives a letter from an attorney with a certified court order showing that Mayra was judicially declared incompetent 3 years ago. **Mayra was judicially declared incompetent three years ago. Any contract entered by her would be void. Sally does not have a contract with anyone to sell her house.**

Exercise 4: Nevada Offer and Acceptance Completion and Analysis

Exercise 4 Synopsis: In this exercise, you will transfer transaction data of a fictional conveyance into a blank sales contract form. Then you will complete several questions relating to the data.

Exercise 4: Instructions: Read the case study data provided and transfer it over to the blank sales contract required. Then, read and answer the questions following the form.

Case Study Data

On November 1, 2021 Seller Sally, represented by Sam the Broker for We Sell Em Fast, and Brian Buyer, represented by Broker Bianca of Down and Dirty Realty, entered a Residential Offer and Acceptance Agreement for the sale of Sally's house pursuant to the following terms and conditions. Complete the sample O&A. Do not leave any blanks. If a term does not apply put "N/A".

- Seller: Sally Seller
- Seller Broker Sam's address: 999 Pretty Solid Rd., Excitement, NV 89xxx. phone 555-555-5553
- Buyer: Brian Buyer
- Broker: Broker Bianca
- Buyer Broker Bianca's address: 4321 Desert Dr., Bliss, NV 89xxx ph. 555-555-5554, email Bob@wesellfast.com
- No salesperson involved
- Earnest money deposit $1,000
- Balance of down payment from buyer funds, proof of funds within 10 days
- Buyer to obtain conventional, 80% of purchase price, 30-year loan, maximum interest 3%
- Total purchase price $450,000
- Buyer to lock loan terms within 10 days
- APN xxx-xx-xxx
- Residential property
- Property and seller address: 1234 Wonderful Lane, Bliss, NV 89xxx ph. 555-555-5555 email Sally@seller.com
- Close of Escrow 12/1/2021
- Broker compensation 5%
- Selling broker compensation 2%
- Loan contingency removal waived
- Appraisal contingency included, buyer to pay for appraisal, reappraisal fee by buyer
- Not contingent on sale of other property
- Seller to buy Owner's Title insurance, buyer to pay lender's policy, buyer to pay for any additional coverage
- Buyer selects home warranty, seller pays
- Oil and propane are included in the purchase price
- Buyer to pay for any re-inspections
- Seller can pursue actual damages if buyer defaults
- Buyer to paid for all inspections requested. No survey is required. The property does not have a well, septic system, fire place, other wood burning system, or oil tank.
- Buyer is waiving a radon inspection.
- Buyer can obtain all other inspections.

Blank Contract:

RESIDENTIAL OFFER AND ACCEPTANCE AGREEMENT

1 RECEIVED FROM _____
2 _____ (BUYER),
3 the amount set forth below as the EARNEST MONEY DEPOSIT on account of the PURCHASE PRICE OF
4 $ _____ for the real property commonly described as
5 _____, situated in the ❑ City OR ❑ Unincorporated Area of
6 _____, County of _____, State of Nevada, APN _____ (Property)
7 legal description shall be supplied in escrow. BUYER ❑ does, ❑ does not intend to occupy the Property as a residence.
8
9 **EARNEST MONEY DEPOSIT (EMD)**   Evidenced by ❑ Check or ❑ other _____
10 payable to _____, held uncashed until acceptance and then deposited
11 **within one (1) business day** of Acceptance with _____. $ _____
12 Authorized escrow holder to be selected by ❑ BUYER ❑ SELLER.
13
14 **BALANCE OF CASH DOWN PAYMENT** (not including closing costs) $ _____
15 Source of down payment _____.
16
17 **CASH PURCHASE**   BUYER to provide evidence, satisfactory to SELLER, of sufficient cash
18 available to complete this purchase within _____ days of Acceptance.
19
20 **NEW FIRST LOAN**: TYPE ❑ Conventional ❑ FHA ❑ VA ❑ Rural ❑ Private $ _____
21 ❑ Fixed Rate for _____ years. Interest not to exceed _____ %.
22 ❑ Adjustable Rate for _____ years. Initial Interest not to exceed _____ % maximum lifetime rate
23 not to exceed _____ %.
24
25 **NEW SECOND LOAN**: TYPE ❑ Conventional ❑ Private
26 ❑ Other _____ $ _____
27 ❑ Fixed Rate for _____ years. Interest not to exceed _____ %.
28 ❑ Adjustable Rate for _____ years. Initial Interest not to exceed _____ % maximum lifetime rate
29 not to exceed _____ %.
30
31 **BUYER** to lock loan terms within _____ days of Acceptance or BUYER agrees to pay prevailing rates.
32
33 **BUYER** to pay discount points not to exceed _____ %. SELLER to pay discount points not to
34 exceed _____ %. Any reduction in discount points at closing to be allocated proportionately.
35 Loan origination fee not to exceed _____ paid by ❑ BUYER ❑ SELLER.
36 **SELLER** agrees to pay up to $ _____ in loan fees that BUYER cannot pay pursuant
37 to FHA or VA regulation.
38 All remaining loan fees shall be paid as required by law, ordinance and/or regulation.
39
40 **OTHER** (Specify in Additional Terms and Conditions or Financing Addendum): $ _____
41
42 **TOTAL PURCHASE PRICE** in the sum of (not including closing costs): $ _____
43
44 **CLOSING**   Close of Escrow (COE) to be on _____. Unless otherwise agreed upon
45 in writing, COE shall not change from the originally agreed upon date. The parties shall deposit, with the authorized escrow
46 holder, all funds and instruments necessary to complete the transaction in accordance with the terms in this Agreement.

Address _____

Buyer [_____/_____/_____] and Seller [_____/_____/_____] have read this page.

ROA Page 1 of 10   This copyright protected form was created by members of RSAR and SNR.   RSAR© 01/21
                                                                                                                      ROA 1/10

1 **DEFINITIONS** BROKER means cooperating Brokers and all Licensees. DAYS means calendar days unless otherwise
2 specified. In computing any period of time prescribed under this Agreement, the day of the event from which the designated
3 period of time begins to run shall not be included. The last day of the period so computed shall be included. BUSINESS
4 DAY means a day other than Saturday, Sunday, or legal holiday recognized in the state of Nevada. ACCEPTANCE or
5 DATE OF ACCEPTANCE means the date on which this Agreement and any other counter offers are fully executed and
6 delivered. DELIVERY or RECEIPT means personal delivery, transmission by Facsimile (Fax), electronic delivery, or
7 certified mail to BUYER, SELLER, Broker, or other representative. In the event of Fax, delivery shall be deemed to have
8 occurred at the time noted on the confirmation sheet generated by the sender's Fax. In the event of certified mail, delivery
9 and receipt shall be deemed to have occurred three (3) days following the date of mailing evidenced by the postmark on the
10 envelope containing the delivered material. In the event of electronic delivery, delivery and receipt shall be deemed to have
11 occurred as set forth in Nevada Revised Statutes (NRS) 719.320.
12
13 **COUNTERPARTS AND SIGNATURES** BUYER and SELLER acknowledge and agree this Agreement may be
14 executed in counterparts, each of which shall be deemed an original and all of which together shall constitute one and the
15 same instrument. BUYER and SELLER agree that this Agreement may be conducted by electronic delivery, and signatures
16 so transmitted shall be acceptable for all purposes. Signatures transmitted by electronic delivery shall be deemed original
17 signatures.
18
19 **LOAN APPLICATION REQUIREMENT (BUYER initial required if applying for a Loan)**
20 [_____/_____/_____/_____] Within five (5) business days of Acceptance, BUYER agrees to (1) submit a
21 completed loan application, including all documentation, to a lender of BUYER choice and (2) furnish a pre-approval letter
22 to SELLER based upon a standard factual credit report, acceptable debt to income ratios and sufficient funds to complete the
23 transaction and (3) agrees to authorize ordering of the appraisal. If BUYER fails to complete any of the above requirements,
24 BUYER is in default and SELLER may terminate this Agreement within two (2) business days and EMD shall be returned
25 to BUYER less BUYER incurred expenses.
26
27 **LOAN CONTINGENCY REMOVAL (BUYER Initial Required)**
28   Included   Waived
29 [_____/_____/_____/_____]   [_____/_____/_____/_____]   Within _____ days of
30 Acceptance, BUYER shall remove the loan contingency.
31
32 BUYER consents to the lender's release of loan status and conditions of approval to SELLER and Brokers. SELLER has no
33 obligation to cooperate with BUYER's effort to obtain any financing other than as specified in this Agreement.
34
35 **APPRAISAL CONTINGENCY (BUYER Initial Required)**
36   Included   Waived
37 [_____/_____/_____/_____]   [_____/_____/_____/_____]   The Appraisal fee is to be paid
38 by ❑ BUYER ❑ SELLER ❑ split equally ❑ other _____.
39 If the appraisal does not meet or exceed the purchase price or there are appraisal conditions, BUYER has the right to
40 exercise one of the following options within the contingency period:
41   (A) proceed with the transaction without regard to the amount of the appraised valuation or appraisal conditions; or
42   (B) renegotiate with the SELLER, provided that if such renegotiation is not successful within 3 business days, then either
43   party may terminate this Agreement upon written notice and EMD shall be returned to BUYER less BUYER incurred
44   expenses; or
45   (C) terminate this Agreement.
46 Parties acknowledge that FHA and VA guidelines may supersede this provision.
47 Any required appraisal re-inspections shall be paid by ❑ BUYER ❑ SELLER ❑ split equally ❑ other _____.
48
49 **APPRAISAL CONTINGENCY REMOVAL** Within _____ days of Acceptance, BUYER shall remove the appraisal
50 contingency.

Address _____

Buyer [_____/_____/_____/_____] and Seller [_____/_____/_____/_____] have read this page.
ROA Page 2 of 10   This copyright protected form was created by members of RSAR and SNR.   RSAR© 01/21
                                                                                                          ROA 2/10

1 CONTINGENT ON SALE AND CONVEYANCE OF OTHER PROPERTY
2 ❏ This Agreement **IS NOT** contingent upon the sale and conveyance of BUYER's property;
3 **OR**
4 ❏ This Agreement **IS** contingent upon the sale and conveyance of BUYER's property described as
5 _____. BUYER to select option **A** or **B**.
6   A.   ❏ BUYER's property is in escrow scheduled to close on or before _____. The sale of
7   BUYER's property is not contingent on the sale and conveyance of a third party's property.
8   **OR**
9   ❏ BUYER's property is in escrow scheduled to close on or before _____. The sale of
10   BUYER's property is contingent on the sale and conveyance of a third party's property.
11 B.   ❏ BUYER's property is currently listed in the MLS System by a REALTOR®.
12   **OR**
13   ❏ BUYER's property shall be listed within _____ days in the MLS System by a REALTOR®.
14   If BUYER's property does not obtain an accepted offer within _____ days of this Acceptance with a
15   scheduled closing on or before _____, then this Agreement shall terminate unless
16   BUYER and SELLER otherwise agree in writing. BUYER shall not accept an offer contingent on the sale of
17   a third party's property without SELLER's written approval. If BUYER accepts an offer contingent on the
18   sale of a third party's property without SELLER's written approval, SELLER may terminate this Agreement
19   and retain BUYER's EMD.
20
21 SELLER shall have the right to continue to offer this Property for sale and accept written backup offers only, subject to
22 BUYER's rights under this Agreement. If escrow on BUYER's property does not close on or before _____,
23 this Agreement shall terminate, unless BUYER and SELLER otherwise agree in writing, and the parties agree to cancel the
24 escrow and return the EMD to BUYER less BUYER incurred expenses.
25
26 BUYER shall provide information regarding the listing, the escrow, and related escrows for the contingent property,
27 including but not limited to, the closing date, loan status, inspections, and additional contingencies on BUYER's property
28 within _____ days of each event. BUYER authorizes SELLER and Brokers to obtain updates on BUYER's listing or
29 escrow.
30
31 If any of the contingencies in the Contingent on Sale and Conveyance of Other Property section are not satisfied, SELLER
32 reserves the right to terminate this Agreement. If SELLER terminates this Agreement, the parties agree to cancel the escrow
33 and return the EMD to BUYER less BUYER incurred expenses.
34
35 **COMMON-INTEREST COMMUNITY DISCLOSURE**
36 The Property ❏ is or ❏ is not located in a Common-Interest Community (CIC).
37 If so, complete the following:
38 SELLER shall provide, at SELLER's expense, the (CIC) documents ("Resale Package") as required by NRS 116.4109.
39 SELLER shall order the Resale Package within five (5) days of Acceptance and deliver it to BUYER upon receipt.
40 CIC Association transfer fees paid by ❏ BUYER ❏ SELLER ❏ split equally ❏ other _____
41 CIC Association set up fees paid by ❏ BUYER ❏ SELLER ❏ split equally ❏ other _____
42 CIC Capital Contribution fees paid by ❏ BUYER ❏ SELLER ❏ split equally ❏ other _____
43 Other CIC Association fees related to the transfer of the (CIC) shall be paid by ❏ BUYER ❏ SELLER ❏ split equally
44 ❏ other _____.
45 The amount of any delinquent assessments, including penalties, attorney's fees, and other charges provided for in the
46 management documents shall be paid current by SELLER at COE.
47 Existing assessments levied shall be paid by ❏ BUYER ❏ SELLER ❏ split equally ❏ other _____
48 CIC assessments levied, but not yet due, shall be paid by ❏ BUYER ❏ SELLER ❏ split equally ❏ other _____
49 BUYER shall have five (5) days from receipt of the Resale Package to review it. If BUYER does not approve the Resale
50 Package, then written notice to cancel must be given within that same five (5) day period.

Address _____

Buyer [_____/_____/_____/_____] and Seller [_____/_____/_____/_____] have read this page.

1 **AREA RECREATION PRIVILEGES AND RULES** SELLER shall comply with CIC (including area recreation
2 privileges) rules regarding the return or transfer of any passes, identification cards, or keys for access to the CIC facilities
3 and general improvements. BUYER shall become familiar with the current CIC facilities and general improvement policies
4 regarding recreation privileges and associated costs prior to COE.
5
6 **VESTED TITLE** Title shall vest as designated in the escrow instructions.
7
8 **EXAMINATION OF TITLE** In addition to any encumbrances referred to in this Agreement, BUYER shall take title to
9 the Property subject to: (1) real estate taxes not yet due, and (2) Covenants, Conditions, & Restrictions (CC&Rs), rights of
10 way, and easements of record, if any, that do not materially affect the value or intended use of the Property. Within two (2)
11 business days of Acceptance, SELLER shall order a preliminary title report, and CC&Rs, if applicable. Within five (5)
12 days of BUYER's receipt of the preliminary title report and CC&Rs, BUYER's objections shall be delivered to SELLER's
13 Broker within this five (5) day period. Should BUYER object to any of the preliminary title report or CC&R's, SELLER
14 shall use due diligence to remove those objections prior to COE. If those objections cannot be removed, BUYER may elect
15 to purchase the Property, subject to the existing objections, or BUYER may elect to terminate all rights and obligations under
16 this Agreement. The EMD shall be returned to BUYER, less BUYER incurred expenses. If SELLER is unwilling or unable
17 to remove BUYER's objections, SELLER shall deliver written notification to BUYER's Broker within ten (10) days of
18 receipt.
19
20 **TITLE AND CLOSING COSTS**
21 ❏ BUYER ❏ SELLER ❏ split equally ❏ other _____ shall pay for a (Standard) owner's policy of title
22 insurance.
23 ❏ BUYER ❏ SELLER ❏ split equally ❏ other _____ shall pay for a (Standard) lender's policy of title
24 insurance.
25 BUYER is aware additional coverage policies are available. All costs associated with additional coverage policies to be paid
26 for by ❏ BUYER ❏ SELLER ❏ split equally ❏ other _____.
27 Escrow Fee to be paid by ❏ BUYER ❏ SELLER ❏ split equally ❏ other _____.
28 Transfer Tax(es) to be paid by ❏ BUYER ❏ SELLER ❏ split equally ❏ other _____.
29 All remaining closing costs shall be paid in the customary manner as required by law, ordinance and/or regulation.
30
31 **OMISSIONS FROM ESCROW INSTRUCTIONS** The omission from the escrow instructions of any provision in this
32 Agreement shall not preclude any party from enforcing that provision. All written representations and warranties shall
33 survive the conveyance of the Property.
34
35 **BONDS AND ASSESSMENTS** (Other than CIC) In the event there is a bond or assessment with a principal balance or
36 that requires settlement in full prior to COE, it shall be paid by ❏ SELLER ❏ BUYER ❏ assumed by BUYER if allowed
37 ❏ split equally ❏ other _____.
38
39 **PRORATION** Any and all rents, taxes, interest, homeowner association fees, payments on bonds, assessments and other
40 Property expenses, assumed by BUYER shall be prorated as of the date of recordation of the deed. Security deposits,
41 advance rentals, or considerations involving future lease credits shall be credited to BUYER at COE.
42
43 **REASSESSMENT OF PROPERTY TAX** BUYER is advised the Property may be reassessed in the future, which may
44 result in a tax increase or a tax decrease.
45
46 **HOME WARRANTY CONTRACT (BUYER Initial Required)**
47   Included   Waived
48 [_____/_____/_____/_____] [_____/_____/_____/_____] A home warranty contract shall be
49 selected by ❏ BUYER ❏ SELLER and shall be paid for by ❏ BUYER ❏ SELLER ❏ split equally ❏ other _____.
50 The home warranty confirmation shall be delivered to escrow and become effective at COE for not less than one year, at a
51 price NOT to exceed $ _____.

Address _____

Buyer [_____/_____/_____/_____] and Seller [_____/_____/_____/_____] have read this page.

1 FIXTURES   All items permanently attached to the Property as of the date of this Agreement including, but not limited to,
2 light fixtures, attached floor coverings, attic fans, central vacuum and related equipment, humidifier systems, drapes/
3 curtains, blinds/shades including rods/hardware, doors and window screens, storm sash, awnings, TV antennas, TV wall
4 mounts, satellite dishes, burglar, fire and smoke alarms and fire sprinklers, built-in pools/spas/saunas and related equipment,
5 solar systems, conforming woodstoves, intercom systems, water softener systems, water and air filtration systems, attached
6 fireplace screens, keyless entries, electric garage door openers with controls, outdoor plants and trees (other than in movable
7 containers), OTHER _____
8 _____
9 _____
10 are included in the purchase price, free of liens, EXCLUDING _____
11 _____
12 _____
13
14 PERSONAL PROPERTY   The following personal property, on the premises when inspected by BUYER is included in
15 the purchase price, free of liens, with no warranty or value implied: _____
16 _____
17 _____
18
19 SYSTEMS AND MAINTENANCE   Until possession of the Property is delivered, SELLER shall maintain the Property,
20 including but not limited to, all existing structures, landscaping, grounds, appliances and systems. SELLER agrees to deliver
21 the Property in a neat and clean condition, and remove all debris and personal belongings, EXCLUDING: _____
22 _____
23
24 OIL AND PROPANE   Any oil or propane fuel existing at the time of Acceptance, allowing for normal use up to COE,
25 shall be ❏ purchased by BUYER ❏ included in the purchase price. If the fuel is purchased by BUYER, SELLER shall
26 contact the fuel company to measure the existing fuel no later than five (5) days prior to COE. The fuel credit amount shall
27 be submitted to Escrow for credit to SELLER. Buyer is responsible for fuel contracts after close of escrow.
28
29 SELLER'S REAL PROPERTY DISCLOSURE FORM (SRPD)   SELLER shall provide BUYER, at time of written
30 acceptance, a completed SRPD which, by this reference, shall be incorporated into this Agreement. BUYER shall return an
31 acknowledged copy to SELLER or terminate this Agreement, in writing, within four (4) business days of receipt. SELLER
32 is required to disclose any new defects between the time the SRPD is executed and COE.
33
34 DISCLAIMER   BUYER understands that the SRPD is for disclosure purposes and is not a substitute for property
35 inspections by experts including, but not limited to, engineers, geologists, architects, general contractors, specialty
36 contractors such as roofing contractors, and pest control operators. BUYER is advised to retain any experts believed
37 appropriate. BUYER understands and acknowledges Brokers cannot warrant the condition of the Property or guarantee all
38 defects have been disclosed by SELLER. BUYER and SELLER acknowledge Brokers shall not investigate the status of
39 permits, location of Property lines, code compliance or any other Property condition.
40
41 ITEMS NOT ADDRESSED   Items of general maintenance or cosmetic nature not materially affecting the value, or use of
42 the Property, existing at the time of Acceptance not expressly addressed in this Agreement, are deemed accepted by BUYER.
43
44 SELLER agrees to provide reasonable access to the Property to BUYER, and inspectors, for inspections and re-inspections
45 and appraiser. SELLER agrees to have all utilities in service the day of any inspection and until COE. If this transaction fails
46 to close, the parties remain obligated to pay for inspections performed as agreed.

Address _____
Buyer [_____/_____/_____/_____] and Seller [_____/_____/_____/_____] have read this page.
ROA Page 5 of 10   This copyright protected form was created by members of RSAR and SNR.   RSAR® 01/21
                                                                                                            ROA 5/10

1 **PHYSICAL INSPECTIONS**   BUYER has the right to inspect the Property, order all inspections, and select qualified
2 professionals including, but not limited to, licensed contractors, certified building inspectors, and any other qualified
3 professionals to inspect the Property.
4 BUYER shall indicate inspections to be included or waived in the list below. The following is not a comprehensive list of
5 possible inspections; therefore, BUYER should add any additional inspections necessary to satisfy BUYER under
6 "OTHER."
7 All inspections shall be completed and copies of all inspections shall be provided to BUYER and SELLER at no additional
8 expense
9   ❑ within _____ days of Acceptance; OR
10   ❑ within _____ days of other contingency: _____
11 Within the time specified above, BUYER shall deliver to SELLER, in writing, one of the following:
12   A. approval of the inspections without requiring any repairs; OR
13   B. approval of the inspections with a Notice of Required Repairs or an Addendum listing all required repairs. SELLER
14   shall respond in writing to BUYER's repair request within five (5) business days of delivery; OR
15   C. termination of this Agreement. If BUYER terminates, BUYER is released from any and all obligations to SELLER,
16   and BUYER is entitled to a refund of the EMD, less BUYER incurred expenses.
17 If any inspection is not completed by the deadline, it is waived unless otherwise agreed to in writing. SELLER is   released
18 from liability for the cost of repairs that inspection would have reasonably identified had it been conducted, except as other-
19 wise provided by law.

20 INSPECTIONS	Included	Waived	N/A	Paid By	
21 PEST INSPECTION	❑	❑	❑	❑ BUYER	❑ SELLER
22 HOME INSPECTION	❑	❑	❑	❑ BUYER	❑ SELLER
23 HEATING SYSTEM INSPECTION	❑	❑	❑	❑ BUYER	❑ SELLER
24 COOLING SYSTEM INSPECTION	❑		❑	❑ BUYER	❑ SELLER
25 SURVEY Type _____	❑		❑	❑ BUYER	❑ SELLER
26 WELL QUALITY	❑		❑	❑ BUYER	❑ SELLER
27 WELL QUANTITY	❑		❑	❑ BUYER	❑ SELLER
28 SEPTIC PUMPING	❑		❑	❑ BUYER	❑ SELLER
29 SEPTIC INSPECTION	❑		❑	❑ BUYER	❑ SELLER
30 SEPTIC LID LOCATION/REMOVAL	❑	❑	❑	❑ BUYER	❑ SELLER
31 FIREPLACE INSPECTION	❑	❑	❑	❑ BUYER	❑ SELLER
32 WOOD BURNING DEVICE INSPECTION	❑	❑	❑	❑ BUYER	❑ SELLER
33 WOOD BURNING DEVICE CERTIFICATION (if req)	❑			❑ BUYER	❑ SELLER

34   Certification requires inspection. In the event device does not meet all applicable codes and/or laws, the cost of its removal shall
35 be the responsibility of SELLER. Stovepipe to be capped off at the ceiling or fireplace to be restored to working order at
36 SELLER's expense.)

37 OIL TANK TEST Type _____	❑	❑	❑	❑ BUYER	❑ SELLER
38 (If oil tank needs to be filled to perform test, BUYER ❑ shall, ❑ shall not reimburse SELLER.)					
39 LEAD BASED PAINT ASSESSMENT/INSPECTION	❑	❑	❑	❑ BUYER	❑ SELLER
40 RADON INSPECTION	❑	❑	❑	❑ BUYER	❑ SELLER
41 OTHER _____	❑	❑		❑ BUYER	❑ SELLER

42
43 [_____/_____/_____/_____] (BUYER Initials) BUYER affirms the above selections.
44
45 **REPAIRS**   SELLER agrees to pay for and complete repairs, in an amount not to exceed the total sum of
46 $ _____. SELLER understands that BUYER has not yet completed inspections, if any. BUYER reserves
47 the right to request additional repairs (1) identified by the inspections; 2) as allowed by Nevada law for SRPD related
48 disclosures or newly discovered defects; 3) or for repairs indicated on the Appraisal Report. SELLER reserves the right to
49 refuse to complete requested repairs in an amount exceeding the repair limit as indicated above, but understands BUYER
50 may have a right to terminate this Agreement. For any repairs completed a copy of all repair invoices and receipts shall be
51 delivered to BUYER prior to COE. Brokers have no responsibility to assist in the payment of any repairs, corrections or
52 deferred maintenance on the Property.

1 **RE-INSPECTIONS (BUYER Initial Required)**
2   Included   Waived
3 [_____/_____/_____/_____]   [_____/_____/_____/_____]   SELLER shall have all agreed
4 upon repairs completed no later than _____ days prior to COE and BUYER shall have the right to re-inspect.
5 Re-inspections shall be paid by ❑ BUYER ❑ SELLER ❑ split equally ❑ other _____.
6
7 [_____/_____/_____/_____]   **SATISFACTION OF CONTINGENCIES (BUYER Initial Required)** All
8 contingencies shall be satisfied according to their terms within the time limits specified, expire according to the time limits
9 specified, or be waived in writing. If BUYER exercises their right to terminate this Agreement under any contingency,
10 BUYER is not in default and is entitled to a refund of the EMD, less BUYER incurred expenses. If a contingency expires, it
11 is waived. BUYER and SELLER shall cooperate in providing written waivers of those contingencies.
12
13 **FINAL WALKTHROUGH**   BUYER shall have the right to a final walkthrough prior to COE.
14
15 **PHYSICAL POSSESSION**   Physical possession of the Property with any keys to Property locks, community mailboxes,
16 alarms, and garage door openers shall be delivered to BUYER ❑ upon recordation of the deed; OR ❑ Short Term
17 Agreement to Occupy After COE; OR ❑ Residential Lease/Rental Agreement.
18
19 **DESTRUCTION OF IMPROVEMENTS**   If the improvements of the Property are destroyed, materially damaged, or
20 found to be materially defective prior to COE, BUYER may terminate this Agreement by written notice delivered to
21 SELLER's Broker, and EMD shall be returned to BUYER less BUYER incurred expenses.
22
23 **LAND USE REGULATION**   BUYER is advised the Property may be subject to the authority of the city, county, state,
24 federal governments, and/or various courts having jurisdiction. These governmental entities, from time to time, have adopted
25 and revised land use and environmental regulations that may apply to the Property. BUYER is advised to research the
26 possible effect of any applicable land use or environmental regulation. Brokers make no representations or warranties
27 regarding the existing permissible uses or future revisions to land use regulations.
28
29 **ENVIRONMENTAL CONDITIONS**   BUYER is advised the Property may be located in an area found to have special
30 flood hazards as indicated by FEMA, avalanche conditions, freezing temperatures, snow loads, seismic activity and/or
31 wildland fires. It may be necessary to purchase additional insurance in order to obtain a loan for the Property. For further
32 information, consult your lender, insurance carrier, or other appropriate agency.
33
34 **WATER METERS**   BUYER may be required at a future date to incur the cost of installation of a water meter and/or
35 conversion to metered rates.
36
37 **WELLS**   Many factors may affect the performance of a well system. If the Property includes a well, BUYER may be
38 required at some future date to incur the cost of connecting the Property to a public water system.
39
40 **ADDITIONAL FEES**   Some areas may have additional fees or charges for the remediation of water systems.
41
42 **SEPTIC SYSTEMS**   If the Property includes a septic system, BUYER may be required at some future date to incur the
43 cost of connecting the Property's plumbing to a public sewer system.
44 At COE, BUYER assumes all future costs associated with water meters, wells, and septic systems.
45
46 **PRIVATE ROADS**   SELLER shall disclose if the Property shares a common road, access driveway, or right-of-way with
47 another property. If a road maintenance agreement exists, SELLER shall provide the agreement to BUYER.
48
49 **WATER RIGHTS**   Water rights, if any, shall be included with the Property unless specifically excluded by deed or
50 mutual agreement.

Address _____

Buyer [_____/_____/_____/_____] and Seller [_____/_____/_____/_____] have read this page.

This copyright protected form was created by members of RSAR and SNR.   RSAR© 01/21
ROA 7/10

1 ADDITIONAL TERMS AND CONDITIONS
2 _____
3 _____
4 _____
5 _____
6 _____
7 _____
8
9 **TAX DEFERRED EXCHANGE**   If BUYER or SELLER request to enter into a IRC tax deferred exchange for the
10 Property, each party agrees to cooperate with the other in connection with the exchange, including the execution of
11 documents deemed necessary to effectuate same. No party shall be obligated to delay the closing. All additional costs in
12 connection with the exchange shall be borne by the party requesting it. No party shall be obligated to execute any note,
13 contract, deed, or other document providing for any personal liability that would survive the exchange. The other party shall
14 be indemnified and held harmless against any liability arising or that has arisen on account of the acquisition of ownership of
15 the exchanged property.
16
17 **VERIFICATION OF INFORMATION**   Any information relating to square footage, land or its use, and/or
18 improvements of the land are approximate or estimates only, and neither SELLER nor Brokers make any representation or
19 guarantee regarding their accuracy. Any oral or written representations by SELLER or Brokers regarding the age of
20 improvements, size, or square footage of a parcel or building, or the location of property lines, may not be accurate.
21 Apparent boundary line indicators such as fences, hedges, walls, or other barriers may not represent the true boundary lines.
22 Brokers are not obligated to investigate the status of permits, zoning, or code compliance. BUYER to satisfy any concerns
23 with conditions that are an important or critical element of the purchase decision. BUYER agrees they have not received or
24 relied upon any representation by Brokers or SELLER with respect to the condition of the Property not contained in this
25 Agreement. The information contained in the Multiple Listing Service (MLS), computer, advertisements, and feature sheets
26 pertaining to the Property are not warranted or guaranteed by Brokers. Errors and/or omissions in inputting information,
27 while uncommon, are possible. BUYER shall be responsible to verify the accuracy of such information. Deposit of all
28 funds necessary to close escrow shall be deemed final acceptance of the Property. SELLER agrees to hold Brokers harmless
29 and to defend and indemnify them from any claim, demand, action, or proceeding resulting from any omission or alleged
30 omission by SELLER.
31
32 **NEVADA LAW TO APPLY**   Nevada law shall apply to the interpretation and enforcement of this Agreement.
33
34 **MEDIATION**   If a dispute arises out of or relates to this Agreement or its breach, the parties are aware the local
35 Association of REALTORS® has a Dispute Resolution Service (DRS) available. A DRS brochure is available upon request.
36
37 **ATTORNEY FEES**   In the event either party is required to engage the services of an attorney to enforce this   Agreement,
38 the prevailing party in any proceeding shall be entitled to an award of reasonable attorney's fees, legal expenses, and costs.
39
40 **CODE OF ETHICS**   Not all real estate licensees are REALTOR(S)®. A REALTOR® is a member of the National
41 Association of REALTORS® and therefore subscribes to a higher ethical standard, known as the REALTOR® Code of
42 Ethics. To receive a copy of the REALTOR® Code of Ethics, ask your real estate professional or the local Association of
43 REALTORS®.
44
45 **PROFESSIONAL CONSULTATION ADVISORY**   A real estate Broker is qualified to advise on real estate. The parties
46 are advised to consult with appropriate professionals including, but not limited to, engineers, surveyors, appraisers, lawyers,
47 CPAs, or other professionals on specific topics, including but not limited to, land use regulation, boundaries and setbacks,
48 square footage, physical condition, legal, tax, water rights, and other consequences of the transaction.

Address _____

Buyer [_____/_____/_____/_____] and Seller [_____/_____/_____/_____] have read this page.

1 **SELLER DEFAULT**   If SELLER defaults in the performance of this Agreement, BUYER shall have the right to recover
2 from SELLER all of BUYER's actual damages BUYER may suffer as a result of SELLER's default, and to pursue any and
3 all remedies available at law or in equity.
4
5 **BUYER DEFAULT**   BUYER must initial <u>only one</u> of the following.
6 If BUYER defaults in the performance of this Agreement, SELLER shall have the right to:
7   A. [_____/_____] (BUYER Initials) Liquidated Damages: SELLER shall have the right to retain, as their sole
8   legal recourse, the EMD. BUYER and SELLER hereby acknowledge SELLER's actual damages would be difficult to
9   measure and that the EMD is a fair and reasonable estimate of such damages.
10 **OR**
11   B. [_____/_____] (BUYER Initials) Actual Damages: SELLER shall have the right to recover from BUYER all
12   of SELLER's actual damages that SELLER may suffer as a result of BUYER's default, and to pursue any and all reme-
13   dies available at law or in equity.
14
15 **THE FOLLOWING HAVE BEEN RECEIVED AND ACKNOWLEDGED BY BUYER:**
16 ❑ Consent to Act
17 ❑ Duties Owed by a Nevada Real Estate Licensee
18 ❑ Environmental Contact List
19 ❑ HUD Inspection For your Protection: Get a Home Inspection
20 ❑ Information Regarding Private Well and Septic System
21 ❑ Residential Disclosure Guide
22 ❑ Wire Fraud Advisory
23 ❑ Other _____
24 ❑ Other _____
25
26 **THE FOLLOWING ADDENDA AND EXHIBITS SHALL BE INCORPORATED**
27 ❑ Common Interest-Community Information Statement "Before You Purchase Property ..."
28 ❑ Lead-Based Paint Disclosure Statement (for properties built prior to 1978)
29 ❑ Open Range Land Disclosure
30 ❑ Residential/Lease Rental Agreement
31 ❑ Seller Financing Addendum (Residential)
32 ❑ Short Sale Addendum to the Offer and Acceptance Agreement
33 ❑ Short Term Agreement to Occupy After Close of Escrow
34 ❑ Used Manufactured/Mobile Home Disclosure
35 ❑ Other _____
36 ❑ Other _____
37
38 **ENTIRE AGREEMENT**   This Agreement and attachments contain the entire agreement of the parties and supersede all
39 prior agreements or representations with respect to the Property not expressly set forth in this Agreement. This Agreement
40 may only be modified in writing, signed and dated by the parties. BUYER acknowledges having read and approved all
41 provisions of this Agreement.
42
43 **ASSIGNMENT**   BUYER may not assign any of BUYER'S rights in this Agreement without prior written consent of
44 SELLER, which consent shall not be unreasonably withheld, conditioned, or delayed. Any purported assignment in violation
45 of this Section shall be null and void. No assignment shall relieve the assigning party of any of its obligations in this
46 Agreement.
47
48 **TIME IS OF THE ESSENCE**   Time is of the essence of this Agreement.
49
50 **SELLER** has agreed, by separate listing agreement, to pay real estate commissions for services rendered, at COE.
51 As published in the MLS, _____% of the accepted price, or $ _____, shall be paid to BUYER's real
52 estate brokerage, _____.

Address _____

Buyer [_____/_____/_____/_____] and Seller [_____/_____/_____/_____] have read this page.

ROA Page 9 of 10   This copyright protected form was created by members of RSAR and SNR.   RSAR® 01/21
                                                                                                        ROA 9/10

1 **EXPIRATION OF OFFER**   Per NRS 645.254, all offers must be presented to SELLER. This Offer expires unless
2 accepted, including delivery to BUYER, or _____
3 on/or before _____ ❏A.M. ❏P.M. on _____ .
4
5 BUYER _____   DATE _____   Time _____
6
7 BUYER _____   DATE _____   Time _____
8
9 BUYER _____   DATE _____   Time _____
10
11 BUYER _____   DATE _____   Time _____
12
13 **BUYER's Representation:**
14 BUYER's Licensee Name _____   BUYER Broker Name _____
15 BUYER's Licensee Nevada License # _____   BUYER's Broker Nevada License # _____
16 BUYER's Licensee Email _____   Brokerage Name _____
17 Phone _____ Fax _____   Office Address _____
18   City/State/Zip _____
19
20 BUYERS Licensee signature acknowledging receipt of EMD _____
21
22   **SELLER'S ACCEPTANCE, COUNTER OFFER OR REJECTION OF AGREEMENT**
23 SELLER acknowledges having read and approved each provision of this Agreement. Authorization is given to Brokers to
24 deliver a signed copy to BUYER and disclose the terms of the sale to members of the MLS or Association of REALTORS®
25 at COE. SELLER has the authority to sell the Property on the terms and conditions stated in this Agreement.
26
27 **TAX WITHHOLDING (FIRPTA)**   Unless the Property acquired for use as a primary residence and is sold for no
28 more than $300,000, SELLER agrees to provide BUYER with (a) Non-Foreign Seller Affidavit, or (b) Withholding
29 Certificate Form from the Internal Revenue Service stating that withholding is not required. In the event none of the
30 foregoing is applicable, BUYER requires a percentage of SELLER's proceeds to be escrowed to comply with the FOREIGN
31 INVESTMENT AND REAL PROPERTY TAX ACT (IRC 1445).
32
33 [_____/_____/_____/_____] SELLER is not a foreign person OR ❏ is a foreign person and may be sub-
34 ject to FIRPTA withholding.
35
36 SELLER shall check one of the following options, and date, time, and sign this Agreement.
37 ❏ **Acceptance of Offer**   SELLER accepts this Offer.
38 ❏ **Counter Offer #1**   SELLER signs this Offer subject to a Counter Offer #1 dated _____ .
39 ❏ **Rejection**   SELLER rejects the foregoing Offer.
40
41 SELLER _____   DATE _____   Time _____
42
43 SELLER _____   DATE _____   Time _____
44
45 SELLER _____   DATE _____   Time _____
46
47 SELLER _____   DATE _____   Time _____
48
49 **SELLER's Representation:**
50 SELLER's Licensee Name _____   SELLER's Broker Name _____
51 SELLER's Licensee Nevada License # _____   SELLER's Brokers Nevada License # _____
52 Phone _____ Fax _____   Brokerage Name _____
53 SELLER's Licensee Email _____   Office Address _____
54   City/State/Zip _____

Address _____

ROA Page 10 of 10   This copyright protected form was created by members of RSAR and SNR.   RSAR® 01/21
                                                                                              ROA 10/10

Completed Contract:

RESIDENTIAL OFFER AND ACCEPTANCE AGREEMENT

1 RECEIVED FROM Brian Buyer
2 _____ (BUYER),
3 the amount set forth below as the EARNEST MONEY DEPOSIT on account of the PURCHASE PRICE OF
4 $ 1,000 _____ for the real property commonly described as
5 1234 Wonderful Lane _____, situated in the ☑City OR ❑ Unincorporated Area of
6 Bliss _____, County of Euphoria _____, State of Nevada, APN xxx-xx-xxx _____ (Property)
7 legal description shall be supplied in escrow. BUYER ☑ does, ❑ does not intend to occupy the Property as a residence.
8
9 **EARNEST MONEY DEPOSIT (EMD)**   Evidenced by ☑Check or ❑ other N/A _____
10 payable to Super Title Co. _____, held uncashed until acceptance and then deposited
11 **within one (1) business day** of Acceptance with Super Title Co. _____. $ 1,000
12 Authorized escrow holder to be selected by ❑ BUYER ❑ SELLER.
13
14 **BALANCE OF CASH DOWN PAYMENT** (not including closing costs) $ 89,000
15 Source of down payment Buyer _____.
16
17 **CASH PURCHASE**   BUYER to provide evidence, satisfactory to SELLER, of sufficient cash
18 available to complete this purchase within 10 days of Acceptance.
19
20 **NEW FIRST LOAN:** TYPE ☑ Conventional ❑ FHA ❑ VA ❑ Rural ❑ Private $ 360,000
21 ☑ Fixed Rate for 30 years. Interest not to exceed 3 %.
22 ❑ Adjustable Rate for N/A years. Initial Interest not to exceed N/A % maximum lifetime rate
23 not to exceed N/A %.
24
25 **NEW SECOND LOAN:** TYPE ❑ Conventional ❑ Private
26 ❑ Other N/A _____ $ N/A
27 ❑ Fixed Rate for N/A years. Interest not to exceed N/A %.
28 ❑ Adjustable Rate for N/A years. Initial Interest not to exceed N/A % maximum lifetime rate
29 not to exceed N/A %.
30
31 **BUYER** to lock loan terms within 10 days of Acceptance or BUYER agrees to pay prevailing rates.
32
33 **BUYER** to pay discount points not to exceed N/A %. SELLER to pay discount points not to
34 exceed N/A %. Any reduction in discount points at closing to be allocated proportionately.
35 Loan origination fee not to exceed N/A paid by ❑ BUYER ❑ SELLER.
36 **SELLER** agrees to pay up to $ N/A in loan fees that BUYER cannot pay pursuant
37 to FHA or VA regulation.
38 All remaining loan fees shall be paid as required by law, ordinance and/or regulation.
39
40 **OTHER** (Specify in Additional Terms and Conditions or Financing Addendum): $ N/A
41
42 **TOTAL PURCHASE PRICE** in the sum of (not including closing costs): $ 450,000
43
44 **CLOSING**   Close of Escrow (COE) to be on December 10, 2021 _____. Unless otherwise agreed upon
45 in writing, COE shall not change from the originally agreed upon date. The parties shall deposit, with the authorized escrow
46 holder, all funds and instruments necessary to complete the transaction in accordance with the terms in this Agreement.

Address _____

Buyer [BB ___/___/___/___] and Seller [SS ___/___/___/___] have read this page.
ROA Page 1 of 10   This copyright protected form was created by members of RSAR and SNR.   RSAR© 01/21
                                                                                                          ROA 1/10

1 **DEFINITIONS** BROKER means cooperating Brokers and all Licensees. DAYS means calendar days unless otherwise
2 specified. In computing any period of time prescribed under this Agreement, the day of the event from which the designated
3 period of time begins to run shall not be included. The last day of the period so computed shall be included. BUSINESS
4 DAY means a day other than Saturday, Sunday, or legal holiday recognized in the state of Nevada. ACCEPTANCE or
5 DATE OF ACCEPTANCE means the date on which this Agreement and any other counter offers are fully executed and
6 delivered. DELIVERY or RECEIPT means personal delivery, transmission by Facsimile (Fax), electronic delivery, or
7 certified mail to BUYER, SELLER, Broker, or other representative. In the event of Fax, delivery shall be deemed to have
8 occurred at the time noted on the confirmation sheet generated by the sender's Fax. In the event of certified mail, delivery
9 and receipt shall be deemed to have occurred three (3) days following the date of mailing evidenced by the postmark on the
10 envelope containing the delivered material. In the event of electronic delivery, delivery and receipt shall be deemed to have
11 occurred as set forth in Nevada Revised Statutes (NRS) 719.320.
12
13 **COUNTERPARTS AND SIGNATURES** BUYER and SELLER acknowledge and agree this Agreement may be
14 executed in counterparts, each of which shall be deemed an original and all of which together shall constitute one and the
15 same instrument. BUYER and SELLER agree that this Agreement may be conducted by electronic delivery, and signatures
16 so transmitted shall be acceptable for all purposes. Signatures transmitted by electronic delivery shall be deemed original
17 signatures.
18
19 **LOAN APPLICATION REQUIREMENT (BUYER initial required if applying for a Loan)**
20 [BB / / /] Within five (5) business days of Acceptance, BUYER agrees to (1) submit a
21 completed loan application, including all documentation, to a lender of BUYER choice and (2) furnish a pre-approval letter
22 to SELLER based upon a standard factual credit report, acceptable debt to income ratios and sufficient funds to complete the
23 transaction and (3) agrees to authorize ordering of the appraisal. If BUYER fails to complete any of the above requirements,
24 BUYER is in default and SELLER may terminate this Agreement within two (2) business days and EMD shall be returned
25 to BUYER less BUYER incurred expenses.
26
27 **LOAN CONTINGENCY REMOVAL (BUYER Initial Required)**
28   Included   Waived
29 [/ / /] [BB / / /] Within N/A days of
30 Acceptance, BUYER shall remove the loan contingency.
31
32 BUYER consents to the lender's release of loan status and conditions of approval to SELLER and Brokers. SELLER has no
33 obligation to cooperate with BUYER's efforts to obtain any financing other than as specified in this Agreement.
34
35 **APPRAISAL CONTINGENCY (BUYER Initial Required)**
36   Included   Waived
37 [BB / / /] [/ / /] The Appraisal fee is to be paid
38 by ☑ BUYER ❑ SELLER ❑ split equally ❑ other N/A .
39 If the appraisal does not meet or exceed the purchase price or there are appraisal conditions, BUYER has the right to
40 exercise one of the following options within the contingency period:
41   (A) proceed with the transaction without regard to the amount of the appraised valuation or appraisal conditions; or
42   (B) renegotiate with the SELLER, provided that if such renegotiation is not successful within 3 business days, then either
43   party may terminate this Agreement upon written notice and EMD shall be returned to BUYER less BUYER incurred
44   expenses; or
45   (C) terminate this Agreement.
46 Parties acknowledge that FHA and VA guidelines may supersede this provision.
47 Any required appraisal re-inspections shall be paid by ☑ BUYER ❑ SELLER ❑ split equally ❑ other _____.
48
49 **APPRAISAL CONTINGENCY REMOVAL** Within _____ days of Acceptance, BUYER shall remove the appraisal
50 contingency.

Address _____

Buyer [BB / / /] and Seller [SS / / /] have read this page.

This copyright protected form was created by members of RSAR and SNR. RSAR® 01/21
ROA 2/10

1 CONTINGENT ON SALE AND CONVEYANCE OF OTHER PROPERTY
2 ☑ This Agreement **IS NOT** contingent upon the sale and conveyance of BUYER's property;
3 OR
4 ❑ This Agreement **IS** contingent upon the sale and conveyance of BUYER's property described as
5 _N/A_____. BUYER to select option A or B.
6   A. ❑ BUYER's property is in escrow scheduled to close on or before _N/A_____. The sale of
7   BUYER's property is not contingent on the sale and conveyance of a third party's property.
8   OR
9   ❑ BUYER's property is in escrow scheduled to close on or before _N/A_____. The sale of
10   BUYER's property is contingent on the sale and conveyance of a third party's property.
11   B. ❑ BUYER's property is currently listed in the MLS System by a REALTOR®.
12   OR
13   ❑ BUYER's property shall be listed within _N/A_ days in the MLS System by a REALTOR®.
14   If BUYER's property does not obtain an accepted offer within _N/A_ days of this Acceptance with a
15   scheduled closing on or before _N/A_____, then this Agreement shall terminate unless
16   BUYER and SELLER otherwise agree in writing. BUYER shall not accept an offer contingent on the sale of
17   a third party's property without SELLER's written approval. If BUYER accepts an offer contingent on the
18   sale of a third party's property without SELLER's written approval, SELLER may terminate this Agreement
19   and retain BUYER's EMD.
20
21 SELLER shall have the right to continue to offer this Property for sale and accept written backup offers only, subject to
22 BUYER's rights under this Agreement. If escrow on BUYER's property does not close on or before _N/A_____,
23 this Agreement shall terminate, unless BUYER and SELLER otherwise agree in writing, and the parties agree to cancel the
24 escrow and return the EMD to BUYER less BUYER incurred expenses.
25
26 BUYER shall provide information regarding the listing, the escrow, and related escrows for the contingent property,
27 including but not limited to, the closing date, loan status, inspections, and additional contingencies on BUYER's property
28 within _N/A_ days of each event. BUYER authorizes SELLER and Brokers to obtain updates on BUYER's listing or
29 escrow.
30
31 If any of the contingencies in the Contingent on Sale and Conveyance of Other Property section are not satisfied, SELLER
32 reserves the right to terminate this Agreement. If SELLER terminates this Agreement, the parties agree to cancel the escrow
33 and return the EMD to BUYER less BUYER incurred expenses.
34
35 **COMMON-INTEREST COMMUNITY DISCLOSURE**
36 The Property ❑ is or ☑ is not located in a Common-Interest Community (CIC).
37 If so, complete the following:
38 SELLER shall provide, at SELLER's expense, the (CIC) documents ("Resale Package") as required by NRS 116.4109.
39 SELLER shall order the Resale Package within five (5) days of **Acceptance** and deliver it to BUYER upon receipt.
40 CIC Association transfer fees paid by ❑ BUYER ❑ SELLER ❑ split equally ❑ other _N/A_____
41 CIC Association set up fees paid by ❑ BUYER ❑ SELLER ❑ split equally ❑ other _N/A_____
42 CIC Capital Contribution fees paid by ❑ BUYER ❑ SELLER ❑ split equally ❑ other _N/A_____
43 Other CIC Association fees related to the transfer of the (CIC) shall be paid by ❑ BUYER ❑ SELLER ❑ split equally
44 ❑ other _N/A_____.
45 The amount of any delinquent assessments, including penalties, attorney's fees, and other charges provided for in the
46 management documents shall be paid current by SELLER at COE.
47 Existing assessments levied shall be paid by ❑ BUYER ❑ SELLER ❑ split equally ❑ other _N/A_____
48 CIC assessments levied, but not yet due, shall be paid by ❑ BUYER ❑ SELLER ❑ split equally ❑ other _N/A_____
49 BUYER shall have **five (5) days** from receipt of the Resale Package to review it. If BUYER does not approve the Resale
50 Package, then written notice to cancel must be given within that same **five (5) day** period.

Address _____

Buyer [_BB_____ /_____ /_____ /_____] and Seller [_SS_____ /_____ /_____ /_____] have read this page.

1 **AREA RECREATION PRIVILEGES AND RULES**   SELLER shall comply with CIC (including area recreation
2 privileges) rules regarding the return or transfer of any passes, identification cards, or keys for access to the CIC facilities
3 and general improvements. BUYER shall become familiar with the current CIC facilities and general improvement policies
4 regarding recreation privileges and associated costs prior to COE.
5
6 **VESTED TITLE**   Title shall vest as designated in the escrow instructions.
7
8 **EXAMINATION OF TITLE**   In addition to any encumbrances referred to in this Agreement, BUYER shall take title to
9 the Property subject to: (1) real estate taxes not yet due, and (2) Covenants, Conditions, & Restrictions (CC&Rs), rights of
10 way, and easements of record, if any, that do not materially affect the value or intended use of the Property. Within two (2)
11 business days of Acceptance, SELLER shall order a preliminary title report, and CC&Rs, if applicable. Within five (5)
12 days of BUYER's receipt of the preliminary title report and CC&Rs, BUYER's objections shall be delivered to SELLER's
13 Broker within this five (5) day period. Should BUYER object to any of the preliminary title report or CC&R's, SELLER
14 shall use due diligence to remove those objections prior to COE. If those objections cannot be removed, BUYER may elect
15 to purchase the Property, subject to the existing objections, or BUYER may elect to terminate all rights and obligations under
16 this Agreement. The EMD shall be returned to BUYER, less BUYER incurred expenses. If SELLER is unwilling or unable
17 to remove BUYER's objections, SELLER shall deliver written notification to BUYER's Broker within ten (10) days of
18 receipt.
19
20 **TITLE AND CLOSING COSTS**
21 ☑BUYER ❏ SELLER ❏ split equally ❏ other _N/A_____ shall pay for a (Standard) owner's policy of title
22 insurance.
23 ☑BUYER ❏ SELLER ❏ split equally ❏ other _N/A_____ shall pay for a (Standard) lender's policy of title
24 insurance.
25 BUYER is aware additional coverage policies are available. All costs associated with additional coverage policies to be paid
26 for by ❏BUYER ❏ SELLER ❏ split equally ❏ other _N/A_____.
27 Escrow Fee to be paid by ❏ BUYER ❏ SELLER ❏ split equally ❏ other _N/A_____.
28 Transfer Tax(es) to be paid by ❏ BUYER ❏ SELLER ❏ split equally ❏ other _N/A_____.
29 All remaining closing costs shall be paid in the customary manner as required by law, ordinance and/or regulation.
30
31 **OMISSIONS FROM ESCROW INSTRUCTIONS**   The omission from the escrow instructions of any provision in this
32 Agreement shall not preclude any party from enforcing that provision. All written representations and warranties shall
33 survive the conveyance of the Property.
34
35 **BONDS AND ASSESSMENTS** (Other than CIC)   In the event there is a bond or assessment with a principal balance or
36 that requires settlement in full prior to COE, it shall be paid by ☑SELLER ❏ BUYER ❏ assumed by BUYER if allowed
37 ❏ split equally ❏ other _N/A_____.
38
39 **PRORATION**   Any and all rents, taxes, interest, homeowner association fees, payments on bonds, assessments and other
40 Property expenses, assumed by BUYER shall be prorated as of the date of recordation of the deed. Security deposits,
41 advance rentals, or considerations involving future lease credits shall be credited to BUYER at COE.
42
43 **REASSESSMENT OF PROPERTY TAX**   BUYER is advised the Property may be reassessed in the future, which may
44 result in a tax increase or a tax decrease.
45
46 **HOME WARRANTY CONTRACT (BUYER Initial Required)**
47   Included   Waived
48 [BB   /   /   /   ] [/   /   /   ] A home warranty contract shall be
49 selected by ☑BUYER ❏ SELLER and shall be paid for by ❏ BUYER ☑SELLER ❏ split equally ❏ other _____.
50 The home warranty confirmation shall be delivered to escrow and become effective at COE for not less than one year, at a
51 price NOT to exceed $ _250_____.

Address _____

Buyer [BB____/_____/_____/_____] and Seller [SS____/_____/_____/_____] have read this page.

1 **FIXTURES**   All items permanently attached to the Property as of the date of this Agreement including, but not limited to,
2 light fixtures, attached floor coverings, attic fans, central vacuum and related equipment, humidifier systems, drapes/
3 curtains, blinds/shades including rods/hardware, doors and window screens, storm sash, awnings, TV antennas, TV wall
4 mounts, satellite dishes, burglar, fire and smoke alarms and fire sprinklers, built-in pools/spas/saunas and related equipment,
5 solar systems, conforming woodstoves, intercom systems, water softener systems, water and air filtration systems, attached
6 fireplace screens, keyless entries, electric garage door openers with controls, outdoor plants and trees (other than in movable
7 containers), **OTHER** _____
8 _____
9 _____
10 are included in the purchase price, free of liens, **EXCLUDING** _____
11 _____
12 _____
13
14 **PERSONAL PROPERTY**   The following personal property, on the premises when inspected by BUYER is included in
15 the purchase price, free of liens, with no warranty or value implied: _____
16 _____
17 _____
18
19 **SYSTEMS AND MAINTENANCE**   Until possession of the Property is delivered, SELLER shall maintain the Property,
20 including but not limited to, all existing structures, landscaping, grounds, appliances and systems. SELLER agrees to deliver
21 the Property in a neat and clean condition, and remove all debris and personal belongings, EXCLUDING: N/A _____
22 _____
23
24 **OIL AND PROPANE**   Any oil or propane fuel existing at the time of Acceptance, allowing for normal use up to COE,
25 shall be ☐ purchased by BUYER ☑ included in the purchase price. If the fuel is purchased by BUYER, SELLER shall
26 contact the fuel company to measure the existing fuel no later than five (5) days prior to COE. The fuel credit amount shall
27 be submitted to Escrow for credit to SELLER. Buyer is responsible for fuel contracts after close of escrow.
28
29 **SELLER'S REAL PROPERTY DISCLOSURE FORM (SRPD)**   SELLER shall provide BUYER, at time of written
30 acceptance, a completed SRPD which, by this reference, shall be incorporated into this Agreement. BUYER shall return an
31 acknowledged copy to SELLER or terminate this Agreement, in writing, within four (4) business days of receipt. SELLER
32 is required to disclose any new defects between the time the SRPD is executed and COE.
33
34 **DISCLAIMER**   BUYER understands that the SRPD is for disclosure purposes and is not a substitute for property
35 inspections by experts including, but not limited to, engineers, geologists, architects, general contractors, specialty
36 contractors such as roofing contractors, and pest control operators. BUYER is advised to retain any experts believed
37 appropriate. BUYER understands and acknowledges Brokers cannot warrant the condition of the Property or guarantee all
38 defects have been disclosed by SELLER. BUYER and SELLER acknowledge Brokers shall not investigate the status of
39 permits, location of Property lines, code compliance or any other Property condition.
40
41 **ITEMS NOT ADDRESSED**   Items of general maintenance or cosmetic nature not materially affecting the value, or use of
42 the Property, existing at the time of Acceptance not expressly addressed in this Agreement, are deemed accepted by BUYER.
43
44 SELLER agrees to provide reasonable access to the Property to BUYER, and inspectors, for inspections and re-inspections
45 and appraiser. SELLER agrees to have all utilities in service the day of any inspection and until COE. If this transaction fails
46 to close, the parties remain obligated to pay for inspections performed as agreed.

1 **PHYSICAL INSPECTIONS**   BUYER has the right to inspect the Property, order all inspections, and select qualified
2 professionals including, but not limited to, licensed contractors, certified building inspectors, and any other qualified
3 professionals to inspect the Property.
4 BUYER shall indicate inspections to be included or waived in the list below. The following is not a comprehensive list of
5 possible inspections; therefore, BUYER should add any additional inspections necessary to satisfy BUYER under
6 "OTHER."
7 All inspections shall be completed and copies of all inspections shall be provided to BUYER and SELLER at no additional
8 expense
9   ❑ within 20____ days of Acceptance; OR
10   ❑ within _____ days of other contingency: N/A_____
11 Within the time specified above, BUYER shall deliver to SELLER, in writing, one of the following:
12   A. approval of the inspections without requiring any repairs; OR
13   B. approval of the inspections with a Notice of Required Repairs or an Addendum listing all required repairs. SELLER
14   shall respond in writing to BUYER's repair request within five (5) business days of delivery; OR
15   C. termination of this Agreement. If BUYER terminates, BUYER is released from any and all obligations to SELLER,
16   and BUYER is entitled to a refund of the EMD, less BUYER incurred expenses.
17 If any inspection is not completed by the deadline, it is waived unless otherwise agreed to in writing. SELLER is   released
18 from liability for the cost of repairs that inspection would have reasonably identified had it been conducted, except as other-
19 wise provided by law.

20 INSPECTIONS	Included	Waived	N/A	Paid By	
21 PEST INSPECTION	✓	❑	❑	❑ BUYER	❑ SELLER
22 HOME INSPECTION	✓	❑		❑ BUYER	❑ SELLER
23 HEATING SYSTEM INSPECTION	✓	❑	❑	❑ BUYER	❑ SELLER
24 COOLING SYSTEM INSPECTION	✓			❑ BUYER	❑ SELLER
25 SURVEY Type_____			✓	❑ BUYER	❑ SELLER
26 WELL QUALITY		❑	✓	❑ BUYER	❑ SELLER
27 WELL QUANTITY		❑	✓	❑ BUYER	❑ SELLER
28 SEPTIC PUMPING		❑	✓	❑ BUYER	❑ SELLER
29 SEPTIC INSPECTION			✓	❑ BUYER	❑ SELLER
30 SEPTIC LID LOCATION/REMOVAL			✓	❑ BUYER	❑ SELLER
31 FIREPLACE INSPECTION		❑	✓	❑ BUYER	❑ SELLER
32 WOOD BURNING DEVICE INSPECTION		❑	✓	❑ BUYER	❑ SELLER
33 WOOD BURNING DEVICE CERTIFICATION (if req.)	❑	❑		❑ BUYER	❑ SELLER

34   Certification requires inspection. In the event device does not meet all applicable codes and/or laws, the cost of its removal shall
35 be the responsibility of SELLER. Stovepipe to be capped off at the ceiling or fireplace to be restored to working order at
36 SELLER's expense.)

37 OIL TANK TEST Type_____	❑	❑	✓	❑ BUYER	❑ SELLER
38 (If oil tank needs to be filled to perform test, BUYER ❑ shall, ❑ shall not reimburse SELLER.)					
39 LEAD BASED PAINT ASSESSMENT/INSPECTION	❑	❑	❑	❑ BUYER	❑ SELLER
40 RADON INSPECTION	❑	✓	❑	❑ BUYER	❑ SELLER
41 OTHER_____	❑	❑		❑ BUYER	❑ SELLER

42
43 [BB___/_____/_____/_____] (BUYER Initials) BUYER affirms the above selections.
44
45 **REPAIRS**   SELLER agrees to pay for and complete repairs, in an amount not to exceed the total sum of
46 $_____. SELLER understands that BUYER has not yet completed inspections, if any. BUYER reserves
47 the right to request additional repairs (1) identified by the inspections; 2) as allowed by Nevada law for SRPD related
48 disclosures or newly discovered defects; 3) or for repairs indicated on the Appraisal Report. SELLER reserves the right to
49 refuse to complete requested repairs in an amount exceeding the repair limit as indicated above, but understands BUYER
50 may have a right to terminate this Agreement. For any repairs completed a copy of all repair invoices and receipts shall be
51 delivered to BUYER prior to COE. Brokers have no responsibility to assist in the payment of any repairs, corrections or
52 deferred maintenance on the Property.

Address _____

Buyer [BB___/_____/_____/_____] and Seller [SS___/_____/_____/_____] have read this page.

1 RE-INSPECTIONS (BUYER Initial Required)
2   Included   Waived
3 [BB   / / /   ]   [/ / /]   SELLER shall have all agreed
4 upon repairs completed no later than _____ days prior to COE and BUYER shall have the right to re-inspect.
5 Re-inspections shall be paid by [✓] BUYER ❑ SELLER ❑ split equally ❑ other _____.
6
7 [BB   / / /   ]   SATISFACTION OF CONTINGENCIES (BUYER Initial Required) All
8 contingencies shall be satisfied according to their terms within the time limits specified, expire according to the time limits
9 specified, or be waived in writing. If BUYER exercises their right to terminate this Agreement under any contingency,
10 BUYER is not in default and is entitled to a refund of the EMD, less BUYER incurred expenses. If a contingency expires, it
11 is waived. BUYER and SELLER shall cooperate in providing written waivers of those contingencies.
12
13 FINAL WALKTHROUGH   BUYER shall have the right to a final walkthrough prior to COE.
14
15 PHYSICAL POSSESSION   Physical possession of the Property with any keys to Property locks, community mailboxes,
16 alarms, and garage door openers shall be delivered to BUYER [✓] upon recordation of the deed; OR ❑ Short Term
17 Agreement to Occupy After COE; OR ❑ Residential Lease/Rental Agreement.
18
19 DESTRUCTION OF IMPROVEMENTS   If the improvements of the Property are destroyed, materially damaged, or
20 found to be materially defective prior to COE, BUYER may terminate this Agreement by written notice delivered to
21 SELLER's Broker, and EMD shall be returned to BUYER less BUYER incurred expenses.
22
23 LAND USE REGULATION   BUYER is advised the Property may be subject to the authority of the city, county, state,
24 federal governments, and/or various courts having jurisdiction. These governmental entities, from time to time, have adopted
25 and revised land use and environmental regulations that may apply to the Property. BUYER is advised to research the
26 possible effect of any applicable land use or environmental regulation. Brokers make no representations or warranties
27 regarding the existing permissible uses or future revisions to the land use regulations.
28
29 ENVIRONMENTAL CONDITIONS   BUYER is advised the Property may be located in an area found to have special
30 flood hazards as indicated by FEMA, avalanche conditions, freezing temperatures, snow loads, seismic activity and/or
31 wildland fires. It may be necessary to purchase additional insurance in order to obtain a loan for the Property. For further
32 information, consult your lender, insurance carrier, or other appropriate agency.
33
34 WATER METERS   BUYER may be required at a future date to incur the cost of installation of a water meter and/or
35 conversion to metered rates.
36
37 WELLS   Many factors may affect the performance of a well system. If the Property includes a well, BUYER may be
38 required at some future date to incur the cost of connecting the Property to a public water system.
39
40 ADDITIONAL FEES   Some areas may have additional fees or charges for the remediation of water systems.
41
42 SEPTIC SYSTEMS   If the Property includes a septic system, BUYER may be required at some future date to incur the
43 cost of connecting the Property's plumbing to a public sewer system.
44 At COE, BUYER assumes all future costs associated with water meters, wells, and septic systems.
45
46 PRIVATE ROADS   SELLER shall disclose if the Property shares a common road, access driveway, or right-of-way with
47 another property. If a road maintenance agreement exists, SELLER shall provide the agreement to BUYER.
48
49 WATER RIGHTS   Water rights, if any, shall be included with the Property unless specifically excluded by deed or
50 mutual agreement.

Address _____

Buyer [BB   / / /   ] and Seller [SS   / / /   ] have read this page.

1 ADDITIONAL TERMS AND CONDITIONS
2 _____
3 _____
4 _____
5 _____
6 _____
7 _____
8
9 **TAX DEFERRED EXCHANGE**   If BUYER or SELLER request to enter into a IRC tax deferred exchange for the
10 Property, each party agrees to cooperate with the other in connection with the exchange, including the execution of
11 documents deemed necessary to effectuate same. No party shall be obligated to delay the closing. All additional costs in
12 connection with the exchange shall be borne by the party requesting it. No party shall be obligated to execute any note,
13 contract, deed, or other document providing for any personal liability that would survive the exchange. The other party shall
14 be indemnified and held harmless against any liability arising or that has arisen on account of the acquisition of ownership of
15 the exchanged property.
16
17 **VERIFICATION OF INFORMATION**   Any information relating to square footage, land or its use, and/or
18 improvements of the land are approximate or estimates only, and neither SELLER nor Brokers make any representation or
19 guarantee regarding their accuracy. Any oral or written representations by SELLER or Brokers regarding the age of
20 improvements, size, or square footage of a parcel or building, or the location of property lines, may not be accurate.
21 Apparent boundary line indicators such as fences, hedges, walls, or other barriers may not represent the true boundary lines.
22 Brokers are not obligated to investigate the status of permits, zoning, or code compliance. BUYER to satisfy any concerns
23 with conditions that are an important or critical element of the purchase decision. BUYER agrees they have not received or
24 relied upon any representation by Brokers or SELLER with respect to the condition of the Property not contained in this
25 Agreement. The information contained in the Multiple Listing Service (MLS), computer, advertisements, and feature sheets
26 pertaining to the Property are not warranted or guaranteed by Brokers. Errors and/or omissions in inputting information,
27 while uncommon, are possible. BUYER shall be responsible for verifying the accuracy of such information. Deposit of all
28 funds necessary to close escrow shall be deemed final acceptance of the Property. SELLER agrees to hold Brokers harmless
29 and to defend and indemnify them from any claim, demand, action, or proceeding resulting from any omission or alleged
30 omission by SELLER.
31
32 **NEVADA LAW TO APPLY**   Nevada law shall apply to the interpretation and enforcement of this Agreement.
33
34 **MEDIATION**   If a dispute arises out of or relates to this Agreement or its breach, the parties are aware the local
35 Association of REALTORS® has a Dispute Resolution Service (DRS) available. A DRS brochure is available upon request.
36
37 **ATTORNEY FEES**   In the event either party is required to engage the services of an attorney to enforce this   Agreement,
38 the prevailing party in any proceeding shall be entitled to an award of reasonable attorney's fees, legal   expenses, and costs.
39
40 **CODE OF ETHICS**   Not all real estate licensees are REALTOR(S)®. A REALTOR® is a member of the National
41 Association of REALTORS® and therefore subscribes to a higher ethical standard, known as the REALTOR® Code of
42 Ethics. To receive a copy of the REALTOR® Code of Ethics, ask your real estate professional or the local Association of
43 REALTORS®.
44
45 **PROFESSIONAL CONSULTATION ADVISORY**   A real estate Broker is qualified to advise on real estate. The parties
46 are advised to consult with appropriate professionals including, but not limited to, engineers, surveyors, appraisers, lawyers,
47 CPAs, or other professionals on specific topics, including but not limited to, land use regulation, boundaries and setbacks,
48 square footage, physical condition, legal, tax, water rights, and other consequences of the transaction.

Address _____
Buyer [BB   /   /   /   ] and Seller [SS   /   /   /   ] have read this page.
ROA Page 8 of 10   This copyright protected form was created by members of RSAR and SNR.   RSAR® 01/21
                                                                                                                             ROA 8/10

1 **SELLER DEFAULT**   If SELLER defaults in the performance of this Agreement, BUYER shall have the right to recover
2 from SELLER all of BUYER's actual damages BUYER may suffer as a result of SELLER's default, and to pursue any and
3 all remedies available at law or in equity.
4
5 **BUYER DEFAULT**   BUYER must initial only one of the following.
6 If BUYER defaults in the performance of this Agreement, SELLER shall have the right to:
7   A. [_____/_____] (BUYER Initials) Liquidated Damages: SELLER shall have the right to retain, as their sole
8   legal recourse, the EMD. BUYER and SELLER hereby acknowledge SELLER's actual damages would be difficult to
9   measure and that the EMD is a fair and reasonable estimate of such damages.
10 **OR**
11   B. [BB _____/_____] (BUYER Initials) Actual Damages: SELLER shall have the right to recover from BUYER all
12   of SELLER's actual damages that SELLER may suffer as a result of BUYER's default, and to pursue any and all reme-
13   dies available at law or in equity.
14
15 **THE FOLLOWING HAVE BEEN RECEIVED AND ACKNOWLEDGED BY BUYER:**
16 ❑ Consent to Act
17 ☑ Duties Owed by a Nevada Real Estate Licensee
18 ☑ Environmental Contact List
19 ❑ HUD Inspection For your Protection: Get a Home Inspection
20 ❑ Information Regarding Private Well and Septic System
21 ☑ Residential Disclosure Guide
22 ❑ Wire Fraud Advisory
23 ❑ Other N/A
24 ❑ Other N/A
25
26 **THE FOLLOWING ADDENDA AND EXHIBITS SHALL BE INCORPORATED**
27 ❑ Common Interest-Community Information Statement "Before You Purchase Property ..."
28 ❑ Lead-Based Paint Disclosure Statement (for properties built prior to 1978)
29 ❑ Open Range Land Disclosure
30 ❑ Residential/Lease Rental Agreement
31 ❑ Seller Financing Addendum (Residential)
32 ❑ Short Sale Addendum to the Offer and Acceptance Agreement
33 ❑ Short Term Agreement to Occupy After Close of Escrow
34 ❑ Used Manufactured/Mobile Home Disclosure
35 ❑ Other _____
36 ❑ Other _____
37
38 **ENTIRE AGREEMENT**   This Agreement and attachments contain the entire agreement of the parties and supersede all
39 prior agreements or representations with respect to the Property not expressly set forth in this Agreement. This Agreement
40 may only be modified in writing, signed and dated by the parties. BUYER acknowledges having read and approved all
41 provisions of this Agreement.
42
43 **ASSIGNMENT**   BUYER may not assign any of BUYER'S rights in this Agreement without prior written consent of
44 SELLER, which consent shall not be unreasonably withheld, conditioned, or delayed. Any purported assignment in violation
45 of this Section shall be null and void. No assignment shall relieve the assigning party of any of its obligations in this
46 Agreement.
47
48 **TIME IS OF THE ESSENCE**   Time is of the essence of this Agreement.
49
50 **SELLER** has agreed, by separate listing agreement, to pay real estate commissions for services rendered, at COE.
51 As published in the MLS, 5   % of the accepted price, or $ 23,000   , shall be paid to BUYER's real
52 estate brokerage, Down and Dirty Realty   .

Address _____

Buyer [BB _____/_____/_____] and Seller [SS _____/_____/_____] have read this page.
ROA Page 9 of 10   This copyright protected form was created by members of RSAR and SNR.   RSAR© 01/21
                                                                                                         ROA 9/10

1 EXPIRATION OF OFFER   Per NRS 645.254, all offers must be presented to SELLER. This Offer expires unless
2 accepted, including delivery to BUYER, or 9/30/2021 _____
3 on/or before _____ ❏A.M. ❏P.M. on _____.
4
5 BUYER Brian Buyer _____ DATE 11/1/2021 _____ Time 2:00 pm _____
6
7 BUYER N/A _____ DATE N/A _____ Time N/A _____
8
9 BUYER N/A _____ DATE N/A _____ Time N/A _____
10
11 BUYER N/A _____ DATE N/A _____ Time N/A _____
12
13 **BUYER's Representation:**
14 BUYER's Licensee Name N/A _____ BUYER Broker Name Bianca _____
15 BUYER's Licensee Nevada License # N/A _____ BUYER's Broker Nevada License # B.54321 _____
16 BUYER's Licensee Email N/A _____ Brokerage Name Down and Dirty Realty _____
17 Phone N/A _____ Fax N/A _____ Office Address 4321 Desert Dr _____
18   City/State/Zip Bliss, NV 89xxx _____
19
20 BUYERS Licensee signature acknowledging receipt of EMD   _____
21
22   **SELLER'S ACCEPTANCE, COUNTER OFFER OR REJECTION OF AGREEMENT**
23 SELLER acknowledges having read and approved each provision of this Agreement. Authorization is given to Brokers to
24 deliver a signed copy to BUYER and disclose the terms of the sale to members of the MLS or Association of REALTORS®
25 at COE. SELLER has the authority to sell the Property on the terms and conditions stated in this Agreement.
26
27 **TAX WITHHOLDING (FIRPTA)**   Unless the Property is acquired for use as a primary residence and is sold for no
28 more than $300,000, SELLER agrees to provide BUYER with (a) a Non-Foreign Seller Affidavit, or (b) Withholding
29 Certificate Form from the Internal Revenue Service stating that withholding is not required. In the event none of the
30 foregoing is applicable, BUYER requires a percentage of SELLER's proceeds to be escrowed to comply with the FOREIGN
31 INVESTMENT AND REAL PROPERTY TAX ACT (IRC 1445).
32
33 [SS _____ / _____ / _____ / _____] SELLER is not a foreign person OR ❏ is a foreign person and may be sub-
34 ject to FIRPTA withholding.
35
36 SELLER shall check one of the following options, and date, time, and sign this Agreement.
37 ❏ **Acceptance of Offer**   SELLER accepts this Offer.
38 ❏ **Counter Offer #1**   SELLER signs this Offer subject to a Counter Offer #1 dated _____.
39 ❏ **Rejection**   SELLER rejects the foregoing Offer.
40
41 SELLER Sally Seller _____ DATE 11/1/2001 _____ Time 4:00 pm _____
42
43 SELLER N/A _____ DATE N/A _____ Time N/A _____
44
45 SELLER N/A _____ DATE N/A _____ Time N/A _____
46
47 SELLER N/A _____ DATE N/A _____ Time N/A _____
48
49 **SELLER's Representation:**
50 SELLER's Licensee Name N/A _____ SELLER's Broker Name Sam the Broker _____
51 SELLER's Licensee Nevada License # N/A _____ SELLER's Brokers Nevada License # B.56789 _____
52 Phone N/A _____ Fax N/A _____ Brokerage Name We Sell em Fast _____
53 SELLER's Licensee Email N/A _____ Office Address 999 Pretty Solid Road _____
54   City/State/Zip Excitement, NV 89xxx _____

Address _____

Exercise 5: Case Questions

Read the following questions regarding the case situation, then answer each question in the space provided.

According to the Residential Offer and Acceptance Contract agreement listed on the previous pages:

1. Does the agreement also serve as escrow instructions?

   _____

   _____

   _____

2. When must the seller deliver the Seller's Real Property Disclosure form to the buyer?

   _____

   _____

   _____

3. What happens to the Earnest Money Deposit if the buyer is not satisfied with one of the inspections and terminates the agreement?

   _____

   _____

   _____

4. Will water rights transfer to the buyer?

   _____

   _____

   _____

5. If a dispute arises between the buyer and seller, are they required to mediate it?

   _____

   _____

   _____

Exercise 5: Answers to Case Questions

According to the agreement

1. does the agreement also serve as escrow instructions?
    There is nothing in the agreement that also makes the agreement joint escrow instructions.

    Typically joint escrow instructions will appear directly beneath the title with a more complete explanation in the body of the agreement

2. when must the seller deliver the Seller's Real Property Disclosure form to the buyer?
    The SRPD is due upon written acceptance. (Page 5, Line 29)

3. what happens to the Earnest Money Deposit if the buyer is not satisfied with one of the inspections and terminates the agreement?
    The EMD is returned to the buyer. (Page 6, Line 15)

4. will water rights transfer to the buyer?
    Water rights will transfer unless excluded by the deed or mutual agreement.

5. if a dispute arises between the buyer and seller, are they required to mediate it?
    No, the agreement makes the parties aware of mediation services, but they are not required to mediate.

SECTION 2 – AGENCY

Chapter 4:

Essentials of Real Estate Agency

THE AGENCY RELATIONSHIP

The most primary of relationships in real estate brokerage is that between broker and client, the relationship known in law as the **agency relationship**. In every state, a body of law, generally called the **law of agency,** defines and regulates the legal roles of this relationship. The parties to the relationship are the **principal** (a client), the **agent** (a broker), and the **customer** (a third party).

The laws of agency are distinct from laws of contracts, although the two groups of laws interact with each other. For example, the listing agreement -- a contract -establishes an agency relationship. Thus the relationship is subject to contract law. However, agency law dictates how the relationship will achieve its purposes, regardless of what the listing contract states.

The essence of the agency relationship is *trust, confidence, and mutual good faith*. The principal trusts the agent to exercise the utmost skill and care in fulfilling the authorized activity, and to promote the principal's best interests. The agent undertakes to strive in good faith to achieve the desired objective, and to fulfill the fiduciary duties.

It is important to understand that the agency relationship does *not* require compensation or any form of consideration. Nor does compensation define an agency relationship: a party other than the principal may compensate the agent.

Basic roles

In an agency relationship, a principal hires an agent as a *fiduciary* to perform a desired service on the principal's behalf. As a fiduciary, the agent has a legal obligation to fulfill specific *fiduciary duties* throughout the term of the relationship.

The **principal,** or **client**, is the party who hires the agent. The agent works *for* the client. The principal may be a seller, a buyer, a landlord, or a tenant.

The **agent** is the fiduciary of the principal, hired to perform the authorized work and bound to fulfill fiduciary duties. In real estate brokerage the agent *must* be a licensed broker.

The **customer** or **prospect** is a third party in the transaction whom the agent does not represent. The agent works *with* a customer in fulfilling the client's objectives. A seller, buyer, landlord, or tenant may be a customer. A third party who is a potential customer is a **prospect**.

Creating an agency relationship

An agency relationship may arise from an express oral or written agreement between the principal and the agent, or from the actions of the parties by implication.

Written or oral listing agreement. The most common way of creating an agency relationship is by listing agreement, which may be oral or written. The agreement sets forth the various authorizations and duties, as well as requirements for compensation. A listing agreement establishes an agency for a specified transaction and has a stated expiration.

Implied agency. An agency relationship can arise by implication, intentionally or unintentionally. Implication means that the parties act *as if* there were an agreement. For example, if an agent promises a buyer to do everything possible to find a property at the lowest possible price, and the buyer accepts the proposition, there may be an implied agency relationship even though there is no specific agreement. Even if the agent does not wish to establish an agency relationship, the agent's actions may be construed to imply a relationship. Whether intended or accidental, the creation of implied agency obligates the agent to fiduciary duties and professional standards of care. If these are not fulfilled, the agent may be held liable

Terminating an agency relationship

Full performance of all obligations by the parties terminates an agency relationship. In addition, the parties may terminate the relationship at any time by *mutual agreement*. Thirdly, the agency relationship automatically terminates on the *expiration* date, whether the obligations were performed or not.

Involuntary termination. An agency relationship may terminate contrary to the wishes of the parties by reason of:

- ▸ death or incapacity of either party
- ▸ abandonment by the agent
- ▸ condemnation or destruction of the property
- ▸ renunciation
- ▸ breach
- ▸ bankruptcy
- ▸ revocation of the agent's license

Involuntary termination of the relationship may create legal and financial liability for a party who defaults or cancels. For example, a client may renounce an agreement but then be held liable for the agent's expenses or commission.

FIDUCIARY DUTIES

The agency relationship imposes fiduciary duties on the client and agent, but particularly on the agent. An agent must also observe certain standards of conduct in dealing with customers and other outside parties.

Agent's duties to the client

Skill, care, and diligence. The agent is hired to do a job, and is therefore expected to do it with diligence and reasonable competence. Competence is generally defined as a level of real estate marketing skills and knowledge comparable to those of other practitioners in the area.

The notion of care extends to observing the limited scope of authority granted to the agent. A conventional listing agreement does not authorize an agent to obligate the client to contracts, and it does not allow the agent to conceal offers to buy, sell, or lease coming from a customer or another agent. Further, since a client relies on a broker's representations, a broker must exercise care not to offer advice outside of his or her field of expertise. Violations of this standard may expose the agent to liability for the unlicensed practice of a profession such as law, engineering, or accounting.

Loyalty. The duty of loyalty requires the agent to place the interests of the client above those of all others, particularly the agent's own. This standard is particularly relevant whenever an agent discusses transaction terms with a prospect.

Obedience. An agent must comply with the client's directions and instructions, *provided they are legal*. An agent who cannot obey a legal directive, for whatever reason, must withdraw from the relationship. If the directive is illegal, the agent must also immediately withdraw.

Confidentiality. An agent must hold in confidence any personal or business information received from the client during the term of employment. An agent may not disclose any information that would harm the client's interests or bargaining position, or anything else the client wishes to keep secret.

The confidentiality standard is one of the duties that extends *beyond the termination of the listing*: at *no time* in the future may the agent disclose confidential information.

An agent must exercise care in fulfilling this duty: if confidentiality conflicts with the agent's legal requirements to disclose material facts, the agent must inform the client of this obligation and make the required disclosures. If such a conflict cannot be resolved, the agent must withdraw from the relationship.

Accounting. An agent must safeguard and account for all monies, documents, and other property received from a client or customer. State license laws regulate the broker's accounting obligations and escrow practices.

Full disclosure. An agent has the duty to inform the client of all material facts, reports, and rumors that might affect the client's interests in the property transaction. The guiding criteria for a material fact is that it is a fact that will affect a party's decision-making process in a real estate transaction.

In recent years, the disclosure standard has been raised to require an agent to disclose items that a practicing agent *should know,* whether the agent actually had the knowledge or not, and regardless of whether the disclosure furthers or impedes the progress of the transaction.

The most obvious example of a "should have known" disclosure is a property defect, such as an inoperative central air conditioner, that the agent failed to notice. If the air conditioner becomes a problem, the agent may be held liable for failing to disclose a material fact if a court rules that the typical agent in that area would detect and recognize a faulty air conditioner.

There is no obligation to obtain or disclose information related to a customer's race, creed, color, religion, sex or national origin: anti-discrimination laws hold such information to be immaterial to the transaction.

Some states (including Nevada) have recently enacted laws requiring a seller to make a written disclosure about property condition to a prospective buyer. This seller disclosure may or may not relieve the agent of some liabilities for disclosure.

Agent's duties to the customer

The traditional notion of *caveat emptor*-- let the buyer beware-- no longer applies unequivocally to real estate transactions. Agents *do* have certain obligations to customers, even though they do not represent them. In general, they owe a third party:

> ▶ honesty and fair dealing
> ▶ reasonable care and skill
> ▶ proper disclosure

An agent has a duty to deal fairly and honestly with a customer. Thus, an agent may not deceive, defraud, or otherwise take advantage of a customer.

"Reasonable care and skill" means that an agent will be held to the standards of knowledge, expertise, and ethics that are commonly maintained by other agents in the area.

Proper disclosure primarily concerns disclosure of agency, property condition, and environmental hazards.

An agent who fails to live up to prevailing standards may be held liable for negligence, fraud, or violation of state real estate license laws and regulations. Agents should be particularly careful about misrepresenting and offering inappropriate expert advice when working with customers.

Intentional misrepresentation. An agent may intentionally or unintentionally defraud a buyer by misrepresenting or concealing facts. While it is acceptable to promote the features of a property to a buyer or the virtues of a buyer to a seller, it is a fine line that divides promotion from misrepresentation. Silent misrepresentation, which is intentionally failing to reveal a material fact, is just as fraudulent as a false statement.

Negligent misrepresentation. An agent can be held liable for failure to disclose facts the agent was not aware of if it can be demonstrated that the agent *should have known* such facts. For example, if it is a common standard that agents inspect property, then an agent can be held liable for failing to disclose a leaky roof that was not inspected.

Misrepresentation of expertise. An agent should not act or speak outside the agent's area of expertise. A customer may rely on anything an agent says, and the agent will be held accountable. For example, an agent represents that a property will appreciate. The buyer interprets this as expert investment advice and buys the property. If the property does not appreciate, the buyer may hold the agent liable.

Principal's duties

The obligations of a principal in an agency relationship concern the following:

Availability. In a special agency, the power and decision-making authority of the agent are limited. Therefore, the principal must be available for consultation, direction, and decision-making. Otherwise the agent cannot complete the job.

Information. The principal must provide the agent with a sufficient amount of information to complete the desired activity. This may include property data, financial data, and the client's timing requirements.

Compensation. If an agreement includes a provision for compensating the agent and the agent performs in accordance with the agreement, the client is obligated to compensate the agent. As indicated earlier, however, the agency relationship does not necessarily include compensation.

Breach of duty

An agent is liable for a breach of duty to client or customer. Since clients and customers rely on the expertise and actions of agents performing within the scope of their authority, regulatory agencies and courts aggressively enforce agency laws, standards, and regulations.

A breach of duty may result in:

- rescission of the listing agreement (causing a loss of a potential commission)
- forfeiture of any compensation that may have already been earned
- disciplinary action by state license law authorities, including license suspension or revocation

AGENCY DISCLOSURE RULES

Traditionally, brokers and agents have disclosed to customers whose interests it is that they are serving. This traditional ethic is now required by law. Agents must know what agency disclosures they have to make, to whom, and when in the business relationship they must make them.

Objectives of disclosure

Disclosure removes confusion about who an agent is working for. It may obviate complaints arising from customers and clients who feel they have been deceived.

Specifically, the requirement to disclose aims to:

- notify clients and customers about whom the agent represents
- inform clients and customers of the fiduciary duties and standards of care the agent owes them
- inform prospective clients and customers that they have a choice in how they are represented
- obtain acknowledgement and acceptance of the disclosure from the principal parties

Recent legislation requires an agent to disclose to all parties the fact that the agent represents one party and does not represent the other. In other words, an agent must inform client and customer that the agent represents the client and does not represent the customer (unless it is a dual agency). An agent must disclose agency relationships whenever there is a transfer of a real estate interest, whether the interest is a fee, partial fee, exchange, leasehold, sublease, assignment, air right or subsurface right.

Seller agent disclosures

Client disclosure. Depending on state regulations, an agent who intends to represent a seller or owner must disclose the import of the proposed agency relationship in writing before the listing agreement is executed. The agent must inform the seller or landlord in writing that the agent will be representing the client's interests as a fiduciary, and will not be representing the interests of any potential buyer. Any subsequent sale or lease contract with a customer should confirm this disclosure.

Customer disclosure. A listing agent must disclose in writing to a buyer or tenant that the agent represents the owner in the transaction. This disclosure must occur before or at the first "substantive contact" with the customer prospect. The disclosure must also be confirmed in any subsequent sale or lease contract.

Substantive contact. Subject to variations in state regulation, "substantive contact" between listing agent and customer occurs whenever the agent is:

- showing the prospect a property

- eliciting confidential information from a prospect regarding needs, motivation, or financial qualification
- executing a contractual offer to sell or lease

Exclusions. Interaction between a seller's agent and a customer is not always substantive. Possible instances that might be excluded from the requirement of disclosure are:

- attendance at, or supervision of, an open house, providing the agent does not engage in any of the contacts described above
- preliminary "small talk" concerning price ranges, locations, and architectural styles
- responding to questions of fact regarding advertised properties

Oral disclosure. If an agent becomes involved in a substantive contact over the phone or in a such way that it is not feasible to make written disclosure, the agent must make the disclosure orally and follow up with a written disclosure at the first face-to-face meeting.

Buyer agent disclosures

Client disclosure. An agent who plans to represent a buyer or tenant must disclose the import of the proposed agency relationship in writing before the representation agreement is executed.

Customer disclosure. A buyer agent must disclose the agency relationship to the seller or seller's agent on first contact. Substantive contact is assumed.

Dual agent disclosures

Informed written consent. An agent who desires to operate in a dual agency capacity must obtain the informed written consent of all parties. Subsequent contracts should confirm the disclosure. "Informed written consent" means both parties have read, understood, and signed an acceptable disclosure form.

Prohibited disclosures. State regulations prohibit a dual agent from making certain disclosures. For instance, a dual agent, unless expressly instructed by the relevant party, usually cannot disclose:

- to the buyer that the seller will accept less than the listed price
- to the seller that the buyer will pay more than the price submitted in a written offer to the seller
- the motivation of any party concerning the transaction
- that a seller or buyer will agree to financing terms other than those offered

OVERVIEW OF LISTING AGREEMENTS

Types of listing agreement

A broker may represent any principal party of a transaction: seller, landlord, buyer, tenant. An **owner listing** authorizes a broker to represent an owner or landlord. There are three main types of owner listing agreement: *exclusive right-to-sell (or lease)*; *exclusive agency*; and *open listing*. Listings are governed both by the laws of contracts and by the laws of agency. It is also important to note that listings are personal service contracts. As such, they are not assignable – since clients may hire a party due to his or her specific skills, which cannot be transferred to another party.

A **buyer agency** or **tenant representation agreement** authorizes a broker to represent a buyer or tenant. The most commonly used form is an *exclusive right-to-represent* agreement, the equivalent of an exclusive right-to-sell. However, exclusive agency and open types of agreement may be also used to secure a relationship on this side of a transaction.

Exclusive right-to-sell (or lease)

The exclusive right-to-sell, also called **exclusive authorization-to-sell** and, simply, the **exclusive**, is the most widely used owner agreement. Under the terms of this listing, a seller contracts exclusively with a single broker to procure a buyer or effect a sale transaction. If a buyer is procured during the listing period, the broker is entitled to a commission, *regardless of who is procuring cause*. Thus, if anyone-the owner, another broker-- sells the property, the owner must pay the listing broker the contracted commission.

The exclusive right-to-lease is a similar contract for a leasing transaction. Under the terms of this listing, the owner or landlord must pay the listing broker a commission if anyone procures a tenant for the named premises.

The exclusive listing gives the listing broker the greatest assurance of receiving compensation for marketing efforts.

Exclusive agency

An exclusive agency listing authorizes a single broker to sell the property and earn a commission, but *leaves the owner the right to sell the property without the broker's assistance*, in which case no commission is owed. Thus, if any party other than the owner is procuring cause in a completed sale of the property, including another broker, the contracted broker has earned the commission. This arrangement may also be used in a leasing transaction: if any party other than the owner procures the tenant, the owner must compensate the listing broker.

An exclusive agency listing generally must have an expiration date. Most states allow either an oral or written agreement.

Open listing

An open listing, or, simply, **open**, is a *non-exclusive* authorization to sell or lease a property. The owner may offer such agreements to any number of brokers in the marketplace. With an open listing, the broker who is the first to perform under the terms of the listing is the sole party entitled to a commission. Performance usually consists of being the procuring cause in the finding of a ready, willing, and able customer. If the transaction occurs without a procuring broker, no commissions are payable.

Open listings are rare in residential brokerage. Brokers generally shy away from them because they offer no assurance of compensation for marketing efforts. In addition, open listings cause commission disputes. To avoid such disputes, a broker has to register prospects with the owner to provide evidence of procuring cause in case a transaction results.

An open listing may be oral or written.

Transaction broker agreement

A transaction broker is in a non-agency relationship with the seller or buyer. The agent is not bound by fiduciary duties to either party. Nevertheless, transaction brokers enter into binding agreements with buyers and sellers to complete transactions. Such agreements may be exclusive or non-exclusive. Like conventional listings, the transaction brokerage agreement binds the principal to a compensation agreement in the event the broker procures a property or a buyer. Typical agreements affirm the nature of the relationship, contain expiration dates, and describe the terms of the agreement, such as the type of property desired or the price a seller deems acceptable. Nevada does not allow transaction brokerage.

Net listing

A net listing is one in which an owner sets a minimum acceptable amount to be received from the transaction and allows the broker to have any amount received in excess as a commission, assuming the broker has earned a commission according to the other terms of the agreement. The owner's "net" may or may not account for closing costs.

For example, a seller requires $750,000 for a property. A broker sells the property for $830,000 and receives the difference, $80,000, as commission.

Buyer and tenant agency agreements

Buyer and tenant agency agreements create a fiduciary relationship with the buyer or tenant just as seller listings create a fiduciary relationship with the seller. Generally, buyer and tenant representation agreements are subject to the same laws and regulations as those applying to owner listings. Thus a representation agreement may be an exclusive, exclusive agency, or open listing. As with owner listings, the most widely used agreement is the exclusive.

In this arrangement, the buyer agrees to only work with the buyer representative in procuring a property.

- an exclusive listing generally must have an expiration date along with other requirements of a valid listing.
- state laws require an exclusive authorization to be in writing

Duties of the Agent. At the formation of the relationship, the buyer agent has the duty to explain how buyer or tenant agency relationships work. This is culminated by a signed agreement where the principal understands and accepts these circumstances. During the listing term, the buyer or tenant agent's principal duties are to diligently locate a property that meets the principal's requirements. In addition, the agent must comply with his or her state agency-disclosure laws which may differ from those of traditional listing agents. This involves timely disclosures to prospective sellers and their agents, usually upon initial contact.

Fulfillment and termination

A listing agreement may terminate in many ways. The only desirable and favorable way is by fulfillment of the contract. Fulfillment results when both parties have performed the actions they have promised to perform.

Agent's performance. An agent performs a listing agreement by achieving the result specified in the agreement. When and if the result is achieved, the agent's performance is complete.

Find a customer or effect a transaction. A listing generally specifies the result to be either finding a customer or effecting a completed transaction.

Finding a customer means locating a party who is *ready, willing, and able* to transact under the client's terms. Effecting a completed transaction means finding a customer who is not only ready, willing, and able, but one who makes an acceptable offer.

A ready, willing, and able customer is one who is:

- amenable to the terms of the transaction (ready and willing)
- financially capable of paying the price and legally capable of completing the transaction (able)

Specific responsibilities. A listing agreement authorizes a broker to undertake actions relevant to achieving the performance objective. Authorized activities usually include the following:

- show or seek property
- locate buyer, seller, tenant, or landlord
- communicate the client's transaction terms
- promote features and advantages of the terms to customers
- assist in negotiating a meeting of the minds between parties

Due diligence. Due diligence in the listing context refers to verifying the accuracy of the statements in the listing regarding the property, the owner, and the owner's representations. Especially important facts for a broker or agent to verify are:

▶ the property condition

▶ ownership status

▶ the client's authority to act

Failure to perform a reasonable degree of due diligence may increase an agent's exposure to liability in the event that the property is not as represented or that the client cannot perform as promised.

Delegation of responsibilities. In the normal course of business, a listing broker *delegates* marketing responsibilities to salespeople. A salesperson may not, however, seek compensation directly from a client. Only the broker can obtain and disburse the compensation.

Compensation

The main item of performance for the client is payment of compensation, if the agreement calls for it. A broker's compensation is earned and payable when the broker has performed according to the agreement. The amount and structure of the compensation, potential disputes over who has earned compensation, and the client's liability for multiple commissions are other matters that a listing agreement should address.

Negotiated compensation. The amount of a broker's commission is whatever amount the client and broker have agreed to. Compensation may be in the form of a percentage of the sale or lease price, or a flat fee. In practice, commissions vary for different geographical areas, types of property and transaction, and services performed.

Procuring cause. Disputes often arise as to whether an agent is owed a commission. Many such disputes involve open listings where numerous agents are working to find customers for the principal, and none has a clear claim on a commission. In other cases, a client may claim to have found the customer alone and therefore to have no responsibility for paying a commission. There are also situations where cooperating brokers and subagents working under an exclusive listing dispute about which one(s) deserve a share of the listing broker's commission.

The concept that decides such disputes is that the party who was the "procuring cause" in finding the customer is entitled to the commission or commission share. The two principal determinants of procuring cause are:

• being first to find the customer
• being the one who induces the customer to complete the transaction

For example, Broker A and Broker B each have an open listing with a property owner. Broker A shows Joe the property on Monday. Broker B shows Joe the same property on Friday, and then Joe buys the property. Broker A will probably be deemed to be the procuring cause by virtue of having first introduced Joe to the property.

Compensation for buyer brokers. Buyer agency agreements stipulate how the agent will be compensated in the relationship. The compensation may be a client-paid retainer fee or a commission contingent upon a completed transaction or procured seller. It is common practice for the agent to be paid by the customer to the transaction, the seller, as opposed to the fiduciary principal, the buyer or tenant. In addition, the agent may be paid by the buyer in the event that the seller or listing agent refuses to offer any compensation to the buyer broker. This might occur, for example, in the case of a for-sale-by-owner transaction.

In addition to the form of compensation and the parties responsible for paying the agent, the buyer agency agreement defines when the compensation is in fact earned and will be paid. Customarily, the commission is earned when a sales contract is completed by the transacting parties. The agent may be entitled to compensation even if the buyer defaults on the terms of the sales contract. Normally, agents are paid at closing or upon the buyer's default.

Causes for termination. A listing may terminate on grounds of:

- *performance*: all parties perform; the intended outcome
- *infeasibility*: it is not possible to perform under the terms of the agreement
- *mutual agreement*: both parties agree to cancel the listing
- *revocation*: either party cancels the listing, with or without the right
- *abandonment*: the broker does not attempt to perform
- *breach*: the terms of the listing are violated
- *lapse of time*: the listing expires
- *invalidity of contract*: the listing does not meet the criteria for validity
- *incapacitation or death of either party*
- *involuntary title transfer*: condemnation, bankruptcy, foreclosure
- *destruction of the property*

Listing expiration regulations. In most states, open listings do not require a stated expiration date. Rather, they expire after a "reasonable" period of time as locally defined.

The other types of listing generally must specify a termination date and may not have an automatic renewal mechanism. Courts in many states construe any listing that has no expiration as an open listing. However, some states make these requirements only of written listings, and may not require exclusives to be in writing.

Revoking a listing

Revocation by the client. If the client revokes the listing after the broker has already earned a commission, the client must pay the commission, no matter what type of listing it was.

If the broker has not fully performed prior to the revocation, the following guidelines apply:

- exclusive right-to-sell: if the property sells during the term of the revoked listing, the client is liable for the commission. If the property does not sell, the client is liable for the broker's actual costs.
- exclusive agency: if the property sells during the term of the revoked listing, the client is liable at least for the broker's costs and possibly for the commission. If the property does not sell during the term, the client is liable for the broker's costs.
- open: if revoked prior to performance, the client is generally not liable for any payment

Revocation by the broker. If the broker cancels the listing or otherwise defaults, the client may sue the broker for money damages.

Check Your Understanding Quiz:

Chapter 4: Essentials of Real Estate Agency

Carefully read each question and provide your best answer based on what you learned in this module. Then check your answers against the Answer Key which immediately follows the quiz questions.

1. In an agency relationship

   a. an agent acts on behalf of a principal.
   b. the servant acts on behalf of a master.
   c. employee acts on behalf of an employer.
   d. the private party acts on behalf of a public party.

2. In a real estate agency relationship, who is the principal?

   a. The broker
   b. The client
   c. The customer
   d. The salesperson

3. To whom does a real estate licensee owe the greatest duties?

   a. The broker
   b. The customer
   c. The client
   d. The brokerage firm

4. What kind of duties does an agent owe to a client?

   a. Fiduciary duties
   b. Common-law duties
   c. General duties
   d. Employee duties

5. Which duty listed below is owed to a client but not owed to a customer?

   a. Duty of confidentiality
   b. Reasonable skill and care
   c. Proper disclosure
   d. Fairness and honesty

6. Which of the following statements is TRUE about a real estate agency relationship?

    a. The agent must be compensated with money.
    b. The person who compensates the agent is necessarily the agent's principal.
    c. Compensation is not required in a real estate agency relationship.
    d. The agent must be compensated by the principal.

7. Which of the following most closely describes "material facts" in a real estate transaction?

    a. Information regarding the materials used to construct a building.
    b. Information that could influence a party's decision.
    c. Unimportant information.
    d. Only Information that affects safety and health.

8. Which of the following has an inherent conflict of interest?

    a. Seller agency
    b. Buyer agency
    c. Dual agency
    d. No agency representation

9. A listing contract is governed by

    a. agency law.
    b. contract law.
    c. ownership law.
    d. agency law and contract law.

10. The parties to a listing contract are a

    a. seller, buyer, and a broker.
    b. seller, and any real estate licensee.
    c. seller and a broker.
    d. buyer and a salesperson

11. John, a real estate broker, has a listing contract with Sam the seller. Bob, through real estate broker Barry, has made an offer on the property. Bob is

    a. John's client.
    b. neither a client or a customer.
    c. Barry's client.
    d. Barry's prospect.

12. The most commonly used listing is a(n)

    a. exclusive agency listing.
    b. exclusive right to sell listing.
    c. open listing.
    d. net listing.

13. Which listing agreement allows the client to hire multiple brokers?

    a. Exclusive right to sell listing
    b. Exclusive agency listing
    c. Open listing
    d. Listing with an option to purchase

14. Which of the following creates a nonagency relationship?

    a. open listing agreement
    b. open buyer representation agreement
    c. transactional brokerage agreement
    d. exclusive agency listing

15. Broker Bernice, along with several other brokers, represents buyer Grace. What must broker Bernice do to earn a commission?

    a. Broker Bernice must be the procuring cause of a sale.
    b. Broker Bernice must exercise due diligence.
    c. Broker Bernice must locate suitable property for buyer Grace.
    d. Broker Bernice must show all property in which buyer grace is interested.

16. Usually, real estate agents are paid

    a. when a buyer and seller have entered a contract.
    b. when a buyer has made a good faith offer.
    c. when all contingencies in the contract have been removed.
    d. at closing.

17. May a real estate broker assign a listing agreement to a real estate broker in another firm?

    a. Yes, if specifically allowed by the brokerage firm.
    b. No, a listing is a personal services contract.
    c. Yes, if it is not prohibited by the listing.
    d. Yes, if the broker has offered separate consideration for an assignment clause.

18. Which of the following is a provision in an exclusive right to sell listing?

    a. The term must be less than one year.
    b. The commission, in a residential transaction, cannot exceed 10% of the purchase price.
    c. The client cannot retain any other brokers for the specific transaction.
    d. The broker can bind the seller to a contract by accepting an offer.

19. In which kind of agreement does the broker NOT owe fiduciary duties to either party?

    a. Transactional brokerage agreement
    b. Open buyer representation agreement
    c. Open listing agreement
    d. Exclusive agency agreement

20. In the context of revoking a listing, a seller

    a. may revoke a listing contract, at anytime without cause or consequences.
    b. may only revoke a listing contract for cause, for example the broker's failure to perform.
    c. may only revoke a listing agreement if the termination date is more than 45 days away.
    d. may revoke a listing agreement but may be liable for damages and expenses.

21. Which type of listing authorizes a single broker to sell the property and earn a commission, but leaves the owner the right to sell the property without the broker's assistance, in which case no commission is owed?

    a. Open listing
    b. Exclusive agency listing
    c. Exclusive right to sell
    d. Net listing

Answer Key:

Chapter 4: Essentials of Real Estate Agency

1. a. an agent acts on behalf of a principal.

2. b. The client

3. c. The client

4. a. fiduciary duties

5. a. Duty of confidentiality

6. c. Compensation is not required in real estate agency relationship.

7. b. Information that could influence a party's decision.

8. c. Dual agency

9. d. agency law and contract law.

10. c. seller and a broker.

11. c. Barry's client.

12. b. exclusive right to sell listing.

13. c. Open listing

14. c. transactional brokerage agreement

15. a. Broker Bernice must be the procuring cause of a sale.

16. d. at closing.

17. b. No, a listing is a personal services contract.

18. c. The client cannot retain any other brokers for the specific transaction.

19. a. Transactional brokerage agreement

20. d. may revoke a listing agreement but may be liable for damages and expenses.

21. b. Exclusive agency listing

Chapter 5:

Nevada Agency and Brokerage Agreements

NEVADA AGENCY RELATIONSHIPS

Legal definition

Brokerage agreement. NRS 645.0045 defines agency as "a relationship between a principal and an agent arising out of a brokerage agreement whereby the agent is engaged to do certain acts on behalf of the principal in dealings with a third party." In this situation, the principal is the brokerage client, and the agent is the broker. The brokerage agreement is a contract that provides for compensation for the broker to provide real estate services to the client.

The statute goes on to explain that no agency relationship is created from a licensee's engaging in communications or negotiations with another agent's client even with the written permission of the other agent.

Thus, if Jeff has a brokerage agreement in place with his client Shirley, Jeff and Shirley have an agency relationship. Don, a broker, meets Shirley at her open house. They start talking about the house, her need to sell it quickly, and whether or not the price is negotiable. Don may even try to convince Shirley to lower the price and include all of the appliances in the deal. Pursuant to NRS 645.0045, even with all of this discussion and negotiation, there is no agency relationship between Don and Shirley. Even if Don had gone to Jeff and asked for written permission to talk with Shirley about the house, there would be no agency between Don and Shirley.

Recognized types of agency relationship

Nevada recognizes three types of agency relationship: single or sole agency, acting for more than one party to the transaction, and assigned agency.

Single agency. Single agency is a relationship wherein the broker represents only one party to a transaction. The agent has a brokerage agreement with that party, and his or her focus is on promoting the interests of that client. The client may be a seller, buyer, landlord, or tenant, depending on the transaction. Single agency is the most common agency relationship and exposes the broker to the least potential for liability issues.

Acting for more than one party to the transaction. Nevada law allows a broker to represent more than one party to the same transaction, a scenario typically referred to as *dual agency*. However, Nevada rejects the term dual agency because it is a term used in common law.

Passed in 1995, NRS 645.251 states that licensees are not required to comply with certain principles of common law, specifically those that conflict with the licensee's duties as set forth in the chapters of NRS. The result of passing the statute was that the prevailing law in Nevada addressing agency duties became statutory instead of common law. Since "dual agency" is not used anywhere in NRS 645, the term does not apply to Nevada's statutory law.

So, while statutory law allows the licensee to represent more than one party to the transaction as long as the licensee fully discloses the multiple representation to each party and obtains each party's written consent, the relationship is just not called a dual agency. To obtain each party's consent, the agent must use the Consent to Act form (discussed later in this chapter) required by the state.

In acting for more than one party to the transaction, it is the broker who is representing multiple parties. The broker him or herself may actually perform the services provided to the parties, or the broker may have one associated salesperson represent the buyer and another associated salesperson represent the seller. Likewise, the broker could possibly represent two buyers looking to purchase the same property and might have one salesperson represent one buyer and another salesperson represent the other buyer. However, it is still the broker who has entered into the agency relationship with both buyers, not the salespersons.

This agency opens the door for a conflict of interest. In the situation where the broker is representing two buyers interested in the same property, the conflict of interest is almost unavoidable.

Assigned agency. To avoid or lessen the conflict of interest in acting for more than one party to the transaction, Nevada law provides what is called an "ethical wall" that allows the broker to assign a separate agent to each client. The assigned agents then work as single agents for their clients, putting their own clients' interests first.

The Ethical Wall protects the broker from liability issues inherent in multiple party representation. The Wall prohibits the assigned agents from sharing the clients' confidential information. It also limits what personal information and documents may be shared between the agents. The Wall requires the clients' files to be kept secured and separate from each other. By complying with the Ethical Wall in an assigned agency, the broker is excused from using the Consent to Act disclosure or obtaining client approval for the agency relationship.

Unrecognized types of agency

Nevada does not recognize *transactional agency*, where the broker agrees to simply facilitate the transaction and not specifically represent either party. Nevada also does not recognize *limited agency,* where the agent agrees to perform only certain acts for the client and, thereby, limits his or her duties and liabilities to the client. Even if the broker and client agree to limit the broker's duties, Nevada law does not allow any duty to be waived, except the duty to present all offers.

Creation of relationship

All agency relationships are created by the broker and the client signing a brokerage agreement. Consequently, completing and signing either the Duties Owed form or the Consent to Act form does not create an agency relationship. These forms are disclosures and not contracts. Each of the forms states that it does not constitute a contract for services nor an agreement to pay compensation. However, the forms are required even in a situation where the brokerage agreement is oral or where the party is unrepresented. The Duties Owed form is not required if the licensee is simply referring a party to another licensee and is providing no other service.

Changes in relationship

If at any point the agent changes his or her relationship with any of the parties to the transaction, the agent must disclose the change in writing to each party as soon as practicable. Since the agent's duties to the client may also change, the agent must provide a new Duties Owed by a Nevada Licensee form (discussed below) to the client and obtain any required written client's consent for the change. If written consent is required, disclosure of the change alone is not sufficient to prove consent.

BROKERAGE AGREEMENTS

Agreement requirements

Oral or written. NRS 645.005 defines a brokerage agreement as "an oral or written contract between a client and a broker" wherein the broker agrees to be compensated for assisting or representing the client in a real estate transaction.

All written brokerage agreements are required to include an expiration date and must have a copy provided to the client at signing or within a reasonable time after signing. All brokerage agreements must include the terms of the agreement, the involved parties, compensation, and time of performance.

Assumption of agency (implied agency). Because brokerage agreements can be oral, the possibility exists that a party may believe an agency relationship has been created based on the licensee's behavior.

The Nevada Supreme Court has found that the assumption of agency rests with the client's reasonable expectations, based on the licensee's statements, representations, and actions. If a licensee provides sufficient advice and the appearance of representation to a party, the party may conclude that the licensee has entered into an oral brokerage agreement with the party and an agency has been formed.

Consequently, licensees must be careful to clarify to the party that no agency exists, especially when the licensee already represents another party to the transaction. In such circumstances, the licensee could be seen as entering into a multiple representation situation without having obtained approval and a signed agreement from all parties.

Agreement types

There are two types of brokerage agreements or representations in Nevada: open agreements, wherein the client may hire several brokers, and exclusive agreements, wherein the seller may hire only one broker. Note that a property management agreement is not a brokerage agreement.

Open brokerage agreements. With an open agreement, the seller may work with as many brokers as he or she wants. The seller may also sell the property him or herself and not pay a commission to any broker.

Open agreements may be oral or written, but all oral brokerage agreements are considered open agreements. All written agreements are also considered open unless the agreement states otherwise or is titled as exclusive. The broker with an open contract receives a commission only if he or she finds the buyer that meets the seller's terms. As soon as the seller accepts one broker's purchase offer, the open agreements with other brokers automatically terminate. If the open agreement does not automatically terminate with the acceptance of the first offer and another broker presents a second offer, the seller could be held liable for owing a commission to both brokers.

Exclusive brokerage agreements. With exclusive brokerage agreements, the client works with only one broker. Depending on how the exclusive agreement is written, the broker may have the exclusive right to sell and will be paid a commission regardless of who is the procuring cause of the sale. On the other hand, exclusive agreements can also be written to allow the client to sell or find a property him or herself and, consequently, not owe the broker a commission.

By Nevada law, the exclusive brokerage agreement must

- be in writing
- be signed by the broker and the client or their authorized representatives
- have a definite termination date with no automatic renewal
- not require the client to notify the broker of his or her intention to cancel the exclusive provisions of the agreement when the agreement is terminated

If the agreement leaves out any of the above required elements, the agreement is faulty and unenforceable. Missing elements can prevent the broker from collecting any earned commission. Failure to include a termination date allows the client to void the agreement and not pay the broker.

Exclusive agreements prevent other licensees from working with or negotiating the sale or lease of a property directly with the client, unless an Authorization to Negotiate Directly with Seller form has been signed. A broker with an exclusive brokerage agreement is required to cooperate with other licensees if and when it is in the best interest of the client. In such cases, the broker would share the commission with the other licensee who was instrumental in selling the property.

Agreement parties

Remember that the agency relationship between the client and the broker arises out of the brokerage agreement. Therefore, the signing of a brokerage agreement brings the duties owed to the client by the licensee, including loyalty and confidentiality. Because of the duties mandated by the agreement and the compensation agreed to in the agreement, brokerage agreements are considered employment contracts wherein the broker agrees to provide certain services for compensation and wherein the broker is an independent contractor and not an employee.

Listing and buyer representation

The two types of brokerage representations in Nevada are the listing agreement, in which the broker agrees to represent the seller, and the buyer representation agreement, in which the broker agrees to represent the buyer.

Listing agreement. A listing agreement is signed between the broker and a property seller who is enlisting the broker's services to market and sell the property. The agreement may be either open or exclusive.

The *exclusive right to sell listing* agreement is the most commonly used. The broker is most likely to be paid with this listing agreement. Even if a cooperating broker assists in the sale, the listing broker still receives a commission. The procuring cause requirement is typically removed from exclusive listing agreements. Exclusive right to sell listings may not be oral agreements and must meet the requirements of any written brokerage agreement.

A sample exclusive right to sell listing agreement can be found online at www.act4u.com/lvre/contracts/c1_List.pdf.

Net listing. A listing agreement can also be written as a net listing, a specific agreement on how the broker will be paid a commission. In a net listing, the seller indicates the sale price (net price) he or she is looking to obtain. The broker strives to sell the property for more than the net price, with the difference being paid to the broker as commission. For example, if Seller Sue wants $300,000 for the sale of her home and Broker Bob sells the home for $350,000, then the $50,000 difference between what Sue wanted and what Bob got is paid to Bob as his commission.

Net listings are illegal in many states because they are seen as a situation where the broker would be looking out for his own interest instead of the client's interest, thereby opening the door for unethical conduct by the broker. Further, many multiple listing services refuse to allow net listings because the cooperating broker's commission cannot be determined. However, Nevada courts have deemed that net listings are alternative formulas for broker compensation and allow the listings in Nevada.

Buyer's representation agreement. A buyer's representation or brokerage agreement is signed between the broker and a property buyer who is enlisting the broker's services to find and purchase a property. The agreement should include the specific provisions of the agreement, the services to be provided, the client's ability to cancel for non-performance, the duration of the agreement, and compensation.

It is common practice in Nevada for buyers' agreements to be oral without much thought to the formal provisions of the agreement because payment typically comes from the listing broker. If the buyer's brokerage agreement is oral, it is an open agreement wherein the buyer can work with several brokers in finding a property. Whichever broker is the procuring cause of the purchase will be paid the agreed upon commission.

Just as with listing agreements, buyer's brokerage agreements can also be exclusive. To qualify as such, the agreement must meet the same requirements as any exclusive brokerage agreement:

- be in writing
- be signed by the broker and the client or their authorized representatives
- have a definite termination date with no automatic renewal, and
- may not require the client to notify the broker of his or her intention to cancel the exclusive provisions of the agreement when the agreement is terminated

DUTIES OWED BY A NEVADA LICENSEE

Sources of the duties

Statutory, common, and case law. When engaging in any activities related to the business of real estate, licensees are required to perform certain duties and are subject to certain responsibilities to clients, brokers, peers, the public, and the Nevada Real Estate Division. The duties are mandated in both Nevada state and U.S. federal law and in state and federal administrative codes. The duties themselves can also be found in NRS 645.252, 253, and 254. However, real estate agency law was created by common law, so where state and federal laws do not define a particular duty, common law prevails. Further, statutory law does not always provide licensees with behaviors to be followed and those to avoid, so the licensee may need to look at the common, or case, law.

For example, statutory law requires disclosure of material facts related to the property but does not define material facts. Case law, on the other hand, finds that material facts are those which would likely affect the principal's decision to enter into a contract or transaction.

"Duties Owed" form

When an agent establishes an agency relationship with a client, he or she is required to provide the client with a "Duties Owed by a Nevada Real Estate Licensee" form, which can be found online at http://red.nv.gov/uploadedFiles/rednvgov/Content/Forms/525.pdf. Informational Bulletin #34, which discusses the disclosure form, can be found online at http://red.nv.gov/uploadedFiles/rednvgov/Content/Publications/Bulletins/IB34_DutiesOwedFAQ.pdf.

The Duties Owed form is required in all agency relationships regardless of the type of representation or the type of transaction (sale, property management, lease, etc.). The form is also required in a transaction where the licensee is the principal. The form includes a section for the client to consent to or reject an agency relationship where the licensee represents more than one party to the transaction.

The Duties Owed form includes the requirements of both NRS 645.252 and NAC 645.637. The form must be filled out in its entirety, signed by the seller and the buyer or the landlord and the tenant, and kept by the broker for at least 5 years. The form is a disclosure and not a contract for services, as clearly indicated on the form itself: "This form does not constitute a contract for services nor an agreement to pay compensation."

Please review the Duties Owed form on the next page:

DUTIES OWED BY A NEVADA REAL ESTATE LICENSEE

This form does not constitute a contract for services nor an agreement to pay compensation.

In Nevada, a real estate licensee is required to provide a form setting forth the duties owed by the licensee to:
- a) **Each party for whom the licensee is acting as an agent in the real estate transaction, and**
- b) **Each unrepresented party to the real estate transaction, if any.**

Licensee: The licensee in the real estate transaction is _____ whose license number is _____ .

The licensee is acting for [client's name(s)]: _____ ,

who is/are the ☐ Seller/Landlord ☐ Buyer/Tenant.

Broker: The Broker is _____ ,

whose company is _____ .

Are there additional licensees involved in this transaction? ☐ Yes ☐ No   **If yes, Supplemental form 525A is required.**

Licensee's Duties Owed to All Parties:
A Nevada real estate licensee shall:
1. Not deal with any party to a real estate transaction in a manner which is deceitful, fraudulent or dishonest.
2. Exercise reasonable skill and care with respect to all parties to the real estate transaction.
3. Disclose to each party to the real estate transaction as soon as practicable:
   a. Any material and relevant facts, data or information which licensee knows, or with reasonable care and diligence the licensee should know, about the property.
   b. Each source from which licensee will receive compensation.
4. Abide by all other duties, responsibilities and obligations required of the licensee in law or regulations.

Licensee's Duties Owed to the Client:
A Nevada real estate licensee shall:
1. Exercise reasonable skill and care to carry out the terms of the brokerage agreement and the licensee's duties in the brokerage agreement;
2. Not disclose, except to the licensee's broker, confidential information relating to a client for 1 year after the revocation or termination of the brokerage agreement, unless licensee is required to do so by court order or the client gives written permission;
3. Seek a sale, purchase, option, rental or lease of real property at the price and terms stated in the brokerage agreement or at a price acceptable to the client;
4. Present all offers made to, or by the client as soon as practicable, unless the client chooses to waive the duty of the licensee to present all offers and signs a waiver of the duty on a form prescribed by the Division;
5. Disclose to the client material facts of which the licensee has knowledge concerning the real estate transaction;
6. Advise the client to obtain advice from an expert relating to matters which are beyond the expertise of the licensee; and
7. Account to the client for all money and property the licensee receives in which the client may have an interest.

Duties Owed By a broker who assigns different licensees affiliated with the brokerage to separate parties.
Each licensee shall not disclose, except to the real estate broker, confidential information relating to client.

Licensee Acting for Both Parties:
The Licensee

MAY [_____/_____] **OR** MAY NOT [_____/_____]

in the future act for two or more parties who have interests adverse to each other. In acting for these parties, the licensee has a conflict of interest. Before a licensee may act for two or more parties, the licensee must give you a "Consent to Act" form to sign.

I/We acknowledge receipt of a copy of this list of licensee duties, and have read and understand this disclosure.

Seller/Landlord: _____	*Date:* _____	*Time:* _____
Seller/Landlord: _____	*Date:* _____	*Time:* _____
OR			
Buyer/Tenant: _____	*Date:* _____	*Time:* _____
Buyer/Tenant: _____	*Date:* _____	*Time:* _____

Approved Nevada Real Estate Division
Replaces all previous versions

525
Revised 11/7/16

Duties owed to all parties

A Nevada licensee acting as agent in a real estate transaction owes the following duties to all parties to the transaction:

> ▸ deal with all parties to the transaction without deceit, fraud, or dishonesty
>
> ▸ disclose material facts related to the property to each party to the transaction as soon as practicable, to include information the licensee knows or should have known through reasonable care and diligence; facts are material if they could impact a party's decision to enter into a purchase agreement or agree to the terms of a contract.

> A licensee may be held liable for failing to disclose information the licensee should have known but didn't and thus has not disclosed. For example, let's say the flood hazard zones have recently changed, resulting in the subject property then being located in a flood zone. The licensee hasn't checked the zoning and so, unaware of the change, he does not disclose the zoning information to the buyer. The licensee can be held liable for failure to disclose this material fact.

> ▸ disclose any source of compensation the licensee will receive related to the transaction
>
> ▸ disclose that the licensee is either a principal to the transaction or has an interest in a principal to the transaction, to include owning or buying the property or being a family member of the owner or buyer of the property
>
> ▸ disclose the licensee's representation of multiple parties to the transaction and obtain written consent to do so from each party
>
> ▸ disclose any changes in the licensee's relationship to any party to the transaction
>
> ▸ exercise reasonable skill and care to all parties to the transaction
>
> ▸ provide the "Duties Owed By A Nevada Real Estate Licensee" form to each client and each unrepresented party to the transaction
>
> ▸ appropriately utilize the Consent To Act form when representing multiple parties to the same transaction

Duties owed to a client

In addition to the duties the agent owes to all parties to the transaction, the agent owes duties that are specific to the client. The licensee's duties as the agent in a real estate brokerage agreement which are owed specifically to the agent's client include the following:

- exercise reasonable skill and care in carrying out the terms of the brokerage agreement
- exercise reasonable skill and care in carrying out the duties included in the brokerage agreement, to include keeping the client's interest first
- keep confidential information relating to the client confidential for one year after the termination or revocation of the brokerage agreement unless the client gives written consent for the licensee to disclose the information, or the law requires or a court orders disclosure

Although the law lists this as one of the duties owed to a client, the law does not define confidential information. Consequently, agents must use common sense and care when determining what information should be kept confidential, to include client information that is directly related to the transaction or could affect the transaction, such as the client's motivation to sell. However, the agent must disclose facts required by law to be disclosed, such as material facts about the property.

Remember, too, that agents' duties are statutory and not governed by common law. Therefore, while common law has no time limit for maintaining the confidential information, Nevada statutes limit this duty to one year after the end of the brokerage agreement. So, if an agent shares such confidential information two years after the brokerage agreement is terminated, the agent has not breached the duty of confidentiality pursuant to Nevada law.

- seek the price and terms for the sale, purchase, option, or lease of the property pursuant to the brokerage agreement or acceptable to the client
- disclose all material facts to the client that the licensee knows
- advise the client to seek advice from an expert regarding matters beyond the licensee's expertise
- as soon as practicable, account for all money and property in which the client may have an interest and which the licensee has received, for example, earnest money received from a buyer

Licensees are not allowed to hold money belonging to a third party. They are required to turn the money over to the associated broker within one business day so the broker can deposit the money into the appropriate trust/escrow account.

> ▸ present all offers to or by the client as soon as practicable

> The seller's agent is to provide written notice of a seller's rejection of an offer or counteroffer to the buyer or buyer's agent. The buyer's agent is to provide written notice of a buyer's rejection of a counteroffer to the seller or seller's agent.

Assigned agency duties

In addition to the duties a licensee owes to his or her client and other parties to a transaction, there is one duty specifically noted that an assigned agent owes to his or her client:

> ▸ non-disclosure of confidential information relating to a client except to the associated broker

This duty exists because the licensees representing both parties to the transaction work in the same brokerage. Consequently, there could be the tendency to share confidential information with an associate licensee. However, because each licensee is bound to his or her assigned client and must act as a single agent to that client, the licensee must maintain confidentiality with and for that particular client. The licensees representing the two parties each may share confidential information with the broker, but the broker is also bound by the duty of confidentiality and must not share one party's information with the other party's assigned licensee.

Duties not owed

Although the agent owes all of the duties previously listed, there are some actions the agent simply is not required to perform. So, unless the agent and the client agree in writing, the agent's duties do not include the following:

> ▸ independently verify the accuracy of a certified inspector or other expert's statement
> ▸ conduct an independent inspection of the financial condition of any party to the transaction
> ▸ conduct an investigation of the property's condition as it relates to the transaction

The agent also has no duty to disclose material facts concerning the transaction itself to all parties. Material facts related to the property are different than those related to the transaction. For example, a property-related material fact might be that the basement is prone to flooding with heavy rains. A transaction-related material fact might be that the seller is willing to accept a much lower price or the buyer is willing to pay a much higher price. The seller's agent has a duty to disclose the flooding issue but has no duty to disclose the seller's willingness to accept a lower price. Actually, the agent is not allowed to disclose that fact because he or she is duty bound to keep such information confidential. However, if the seller's agent learns the buyer is willing to pay a higher price for the property, the agent has a duty to disclose that to the seller even though that is a transaction-related material fact.

Breach of duties

Nevada law recognizes three behaviors that are considered breach of owed duties and can create liability:

- ▶ nonfeasance-- not doing what is required: failing to make required disclosures, failing to account for money belonging to others, etc.
- ▶ malfeasance-- doing what is not allowed: intentionally withholding some offers while presenting other offers, holding money belonging to others rather than turning it over to the broker, etc.
- ▶ misfeasance-- doing what is required in the wrong or negligent way: signing a brokerage agreement with specific provisions and then performing the provisions differently than required, etc.

CONSENT TO ACT; MULTIPLE REPRESENTATION

Nevada allows an agent to act for more than one party to the transaction, or multiple representation agency. Such an agency relationship can be formed by different representations in the same transaction. Typically, the agency consists of a broker representing both the buyer and the seller of the same property. In sellers' markets, the broker may represent two or more buyers who are competing for the same property. In an uncommon scenario, the broker could represent a seller and multiple buyers all tied to the same property.

Consent to Act disclosure form. In a multiple representation agency, the law requires the broker and any assigned agents to perform the same duties as are required of licensees in any agency relationship. Because the law acknowledges the conflict of interest created with a multiple representation agency, the state requires the use of the Consent to Act disclosure form. Regardless of the representation mixture, each party must be given the form and be allowed to reject the multiple representation agency relationship. The Consent to Act form can be found online at http://red.nv.gov/uploadedFiles/rednvgov/Content/Forms/524.pdf.

The form is used to disclose the multiple representation and for the licensee to obtain each party's written approval for the licensee to represent more than one party in the transaction. Once the disclosure of the multiple representation is made, the licensee must obtain the signed consent from each party before the licensee can continue to act as the agent in the transaction. Please review the Consent to Act form on the next page.

CONSENT TO ACT

This form does not constitute a contract for services nor an agreement to pay compensation.

DESCRIPTION OF TRANSACTION: The real estate transaction is the ☐ sale and purchase; or ☐ lease; of

Property Address: _____

_____.

In Nevada, a real estate licensee may act for more than one party in a real estate transaction however, before the licensee does so, he or she must obtain the written consent of each party. This form is that consent. Before you consent to having a licensee represent both yourself and the other party, you should read this form and understand it.

Licensee: The licensee in this real estate transaction is _____ ("Licensee") whose

license number is _____ and who is affiliated with _____ ("Brokerage").

Seller/Landlord _____
                              Print Name

Buyer/Tenant _____
                            Print Name

CONFLICT OF INTEREST: A licensee in a real estate transaction may legally act for two or more parties who have interests adverse to each other. In acting for these parties, the licensee has a conflict of interest.

DISCLOSURE OF CONFIDENTIAL INFORMATION: Licensee will not disclose any confidential information for 1 year after the revocation or termination of any brokerage agreement entered into with a party to this transaction, unless Licensee is required to do so by a court of competent jurisdiction or is given written permission to do so by that party. Confidential information includes, but is not limited to, the client's motivation to purchase, trade or sell, which if disclosed, could harm one party's bargaining position or benefit the other.

DUTIES OF LICENSEE: Licensee shall provide you with a "Duties Owed by a Nevada Real Estate Licensee" disclosure form which lists the duties a licensee owes to all parties of a real estate transaction, and those owed to the licensee's client. When representing both parties, the licensee owes the same duties to both seller and buyer. Licensee shall disclose to both Seller and Buyer all known defects in the property, any matter that must be disclosed by law, and any information the licensee believes may be material or might affect Seller's/Landlord's or Buyer's/Tenant's decisions with respect to this transaction.

NO REQUIREMENT TO CONSENT: You are not required to consent to this licensee acting on your behalf. You may
- – Reject this consent and obtain your own agent,
- – Represent yourself,
- – Request that the licensee's broker assign you your own licensee.

CONFIRMATION OF DISCLOSURE AND INFORMATION CONSENT

BY MY SIGNATURE BELOW, I UNDERSTAND AND CONSENT: I am giving my consent to have the above identified licensee act for both the other party and me. By signing below, I acknowledge that I understand the ramifications of this consent, and that I acknowledge that I am giving this consent without coercion.

I/We acknowledge receipt of a copy of this list of licensee duties, and have read and understand this disclosure.					
Seller/Landlord	*Date*	*Time*	*Buyer/Tenant*	*Date*	*Time*
Seller/Landlord	*Date*	*Time*	*Buyer/Tenant*	*Date*	*Time*

**Contents of the
Consent to Act form**   To comply with the law, the written consent is required to include the following:

▶   a description of the transaction

▶   a statement that the licensee is acting for multiple parties to the transaction and, thus, has a conflict of interest

▶   a statement that the licensee will not disclose any confidential information for at least one year after the termination or revocation of the brokerage agreement unless required to do so by law or a court order or given written permission by the related party

▶   a statement that the party receiving the form is not required to consent to the licensee acting on his or her behalf

▶   a statement that the signing party is giving consent without coercion and that the signing party understands the terms of the consent

The Nevada form contains the required statements and other information:

▶   It's disclaimer-- language at the top of the form states it is not a contract: "This form does not constitute a contract for services nor an agreement to pay compensation."

▶   property and transaction information-- includes the property address and checkboxes to indicate if the transaction is a sale and purchase or a lease; explains that multiple representations are allowed in Nevada, that each party's consent must be obtained for the representation, and that this form serves as that consent

▶   parties and licensee information-- the licensee's information and the names of the parties to the transaction

▶   conflict of interest warning-- explains that licensee is acting for multiple parties who have adverse interests

▶   Disclosure of Confidential Information notice-- explains that licensee will not disclose confidential information for one year after the end of the brokerage agreement unless required to do so; defines what constitutes confidential information

▶   duties of the licensee section-- explains that the licensee owes certain duties to all parties and other duties to the client; also explains the necessary disclosure of material facts and the licensee's duty to provide the signer with a Duties Owed form

▶   no requirement to consent section-- explains that the party does not have to consent to multiple representation and gives three options for parties who do not consent

> ▸ signatures section-- signatures of the parties who consent to the agency; includes language that indicates the signing party understands the consent and is giving consent without coercion

Import of the Consent to Act form. By signing the form, the parties are consenting to the licensee's representation of the multiple parties. If one of the parties does not want to enter into a multiple representation agency, he or she would refuse to sign the consent, as there is no place on the form for the party to reject the agency. The party may then obtain a different agent, represent him or herself, or ask the associated broker to assign a separate licensee to that party.

Licensees must be aware that failing to disclose multiple representation and to obtain written consent is a violation of the law. Consequently, they must also be aware of a situation that appears to be an undisclosed multiple representation. For example, a seller's agent might assist the buyer, resulting in the buyer believing the agent is then representing him or her. The result of this situation would be an undisclosed representation of multiple parties. Unless the agent is careful when interacting with other parties to the transaction, he or she may end up inadvertently violating the law.

A large number of disciplinary hearings brought before the Commission are based on agency disclosure form violations. The forms are not given to the clients or completed correctly or lack signatures, etc. The Commission has determined that failure to correctly execute the forms is gross negligence by the licensee, so each broker should ensure that his or her associated licensees are using the disclosure forms consistently and correctly. Any time there is a change regarding the parties or the licensee, the parties must be provided with, and sign, a new form.

CONFIRMATION OF AGENCY RELATIONSHIP

Oral vs written agreements. Nevada law states that agency is the relationship between an agent and a principal that is the result of a brokerage agreement wherein the signing parties agree the agent will perform certain acts on behalf of the principal in transactions with a third party. So, pursuant to the law, there must be a brokerage agreement for agency to exist.

The potential for a misunderstanding or an assumption of agency is in the definition of a brokerage agreement: an oral or written contract between an agent and a client wherein the broker agrees to provide real estate services to the client in exchange for compensation.

Express vs implied agreements. Agency relationships are typically created by express statements. The client and the broker expressly agree to the relationship through the contract. However, agency relationships can also be created unintentionally, when the licensee's actions lead the client to reasonably assume that the licensee is representing him or her, but the licensee does not intend to do so. Similarly, an implied agency can be created when the licensee, intending to represent the client, acts as though he or she is representing the client, and the client silently accepts the services even though there is no express agreement.

Because the law allows the agreement to be oral, the potential exists for the licensee to act in a way that leads a party to believe or expect that an oral agreement exists and that the licensee is the party's agent. Thus, the client may believe an agency relationship has been created, albeit an unintentional agency.

The Nevada Supreme Court has upheld that the assumption of the existence of agency is based on the client's reasonable expectations. The court looks at the licensee's statements, actions, and representations when determining if the client's expectations are reasonable.

Written disclosure. Consequently, it is important for a licensee to confirm or deny the existence of agency with a party. NAC 645.637 mandates that the licensee clearly disclose his or her relationship with the client in writing to both the client and any unrepresented party to the transaction. The licensee must provide the written disclosure to the involved parties as soon as practicable but before any written document is signed by the client or the unrepresented party. The written agency disclosure must be attached to whatever other document is being signed. The licensee is then to keep the agency disclosure document in the same files as other documents related to the transaction.

The Duties Owed by a Nevada Real Estate Licensee form serves as the agency disclosure, as the top section of the form provides the licensee's information and includes the name of the client for whom the licensee is acting. When the party does the form, he or she is acknowledging receipt of the disclosure, thereby providing the licensee with proof of disclosure lessened risk of liability from an unintentional agency.

WAIVER OF DUTY TO PRESENT ALL OFFERS

One of a licensee's duties to a client is to present all property purchase offers. Although Nevada law does not allow any other licensee duty to be waived, it makes an exception for this particular duty. Pursuant to the law, the client may release the licensee from the duty to present all offers by signing a waiver. This must be done on the mandated Waiver Form (NRED Form 636) found online at the address below. This is the only licensee duty that Nevada law allows to be waived. http://red.nv.gov/uploadedFiles/rednvgov/Content/Forms/636.pdf.

The waiver form includes the following language:

> By signing below I agree that the licensee who represents me shall not present any offers made to or by me, as defined above. I understand that a real estate transaction has significant legal and financial consequences. I further understand that in any proposed transaction,

the other licensee(s) involved represents the interests of the other party, does not represent me and cannot perform the waived duty on my behalf. I further understand that I should seek the assistance of other professionals such as an attorney. I further understand that it is my responsibility to inform myself of the steps necessary to fulfill the terms of any purchase agreement that I may execute. I further understand that this waiver may be revoked in writing by mutual agreement between client and broker.

This language in the waiver agreement releases the buyer's agent from appearing to enter into an agency agreement with the signing seller. However, it still does not give written permission for the buyer's agent to negotiate with the seller. That permission is granted by use of the Authorization to Negotiate Directly with Seller form.

STATE OF NEVADA
DEPARTMENT OF BUSINESS AND INDUSTRY
REAL ESTATE DIVISION

3300 W. Sahara Ave., Suite 350, Las Vegas, Nevada 89102 * (702) 486-4033
e-mail: realest@red.nv.gov * http://red.nv.gov/

WAIVER FORM

In representing any client in an agency relationship, a real estate licensee has specific statutory duties to that client. Under Nevada law only one of these duties can be waived. NRS 645.254 requires a licensee to "present all offers made to or by the client as soon as practicable." This duty may be waived by the client.

"Presenting all offers" includes without limitation: accepting delivery of and conveying offers and counteroffers; answering a client's questions regarding offers and counteroffers; and assisting a client in preparing, communicating and negotiating offers and counteroffers.

In order to waive the duty, the client must enter into a written agreement waiving the licensee's obligation to perform the duty to present all offers. By signing below you are agreeing that the licensee who is representing you will not perform the duty of presenting all offers made to or by you with regard to the property located at:

_____ .

Property Address   City

AGREEMENT TO WAIVER

By signing below I agree that the licensee who represents me shall not present any offers made to or by me, as defined above. I understand that a real estate transaction has significant legal and financial consequences. I further understand that in any proposed transaction, the other licensee(s) involved represents the interests of the other party, does not represent me and cannot perform the waived duty on my behalf. I further understand that I should seek the assistance of other professionals such as an attorney. I further understand that it is my responsibility to inform myself of the steps necessary to fulfill the terms of any purchase agreement that I may execute. I further understand that this waiver may be revoked in writing by mutual agreement between client and broker.

WAIVER NOT VALID UNTIL SIGNED BY BROKER.

_____	_____	_____	_____
Client	Date	Licensee	Date
_____	_____	_____	_____
Client	Date	Broker	Date
Revised: 03/20/17			636

AUTHORITY TO NEGOTIATE DIRECTLY

If a property seller has an exclusive agency relationship with an agent, other agents are not allowed to communicate or negotiate with that seller. Even if the seller has signed a Waiver Form to release his or her agent from accepting and presenting offers, a buyer's agent may not present offers directly to the seller or negotiate terms or price. This prohibited interaction is to alleviate any chance of implied agency. However, Nevada law allows the buyer's agent access to the seller *IF* the seller's agent provides written permission and the seller agrees. Even with the written permission, the NRS definition of agency precludes an agency being created by such communication alone.

The state's "Authorization to Negotiate Directly with Seller" form allows the agent to provide that written permission. The form can be found online at http://red.nv.gov/uploadedFiles/rednvgov/Content/Forms/637.pdf

According to The Nevada Law and Reference Guide (http://red.nv.gov/uploadedFiles/rednvgov/Content/Publications/References/lawguide2014.pdf), the Authorization limits the type of communication between the seller and the buyer's agent to

> ▸ delivery, communication, or facilitation of an offer, counteroffer, or proposal
>
> ▸ discussion and review of the terms of an offer, counteroffer, or proposal
>
> ▸ preparation of any responses as directed

The Authorization form defines "negotiate" as "(a) delivering or communicating an offer, counteroffer, or proposal; (b) discussing or reviewing the terms of any offer, counteroffer, or proposal; and/or (c) facilitating communication regarding an offer, counteroffer, or proposal and preparing any response as directed."

The form explains that additional contact with the buyer's agent may be necessary after the seller accepts the offer to allow the buyer's agent to obtain disclosures and other transaction-related documents. It goes on to state that the seller agrees that the buyer's agent does not represent the seller and there is no agency created or implied by the agent's additional contact with the seller.

Purposes of the Authorization to Negotiate.... Form. This form serves several purposes. First, it gives the buyer's agent permission to communicate directly with the seller. Second, it discloses to the seller that there is no agency relationship between the seller and the buyer's agent, thereby protecting that agent from the appearance of entering into an undisclosed multiple representation agency or an implied agency. Third, it advises the seller to seek advice from his or her broker, financial adviser, or legal counsel.

STATE OF NEVADA
DEPARTMENT OF BUSINESS AND INDUSTRY
REAL ESTATE DIVISION

3300 W. Sahara Ave., Suite 350, Las Vegas, Nevada 89102 * (702) 486-4033
e-mail: realest@red.nv.gov * http://red.nv.gov/

AUTHORIZATION TO NEGOTIATE
DIRECTLY WITH SELLER

Nevada law permits a real estate licensee to negotiate a sale or lease directly with the seller or lessor with written permission from the listing broker. This form grants that permission with respect to the below-named Seller(s) and the listed property.

• Seller agrees, and the Seller's broker authorizes, that a Buyer's agent or broker may present offers (including subsequent counteroffers) and negotiate directly with the Seller.

• "Negotiate" means (a) delivering or communicating an offer, counteroffer, or proposal; (b) discussing or reviewing the terms of any offer, counteroffer, or proposal; and/or (c) facilitating communication regarding an offer, counteroffer, or proposal and preparing any response as directed.

• Seller understands and agrees that, after accepting an offer, additional contact from the Buyer's agent may be required to obtain disclosures and other documents related to the transaction.

• Seller acknowledges and agrees that Buyer's agent does not represent the Seller, and negotiations pursuant to this authorization do not create or imply an agency relationship between the Buyer's agent and the Seller. Seller understands that he/she should seek advice from Seller's broker and/or financial advisers or legal counsel.

• Seller acknowledges that Seller's broker will provide a copy of this authorization to the Buyer's agent or broker upon request, prior to presenting an offer.

Seller's Name(s): _____

Seller's Signature(s): _____   _____/_____
                                                              Date   Time

Property Address: _____

City: _____ Zip: _____ Contract Listing Date: _____

Company Name: _____

Seller's Agent Name: _____ Signature: _____

                                                              _____/_____
                                                              Date   Time

Seller's Broker Name: _____ Signature: _____

                                                              _____/_____
                                                              Date   Time

Revised: 03/20/17   637

LISTING AGREEMENT CLAUSES

A written listing, particularly an exclusive, is a formal contract which contains the entirety of all agreements between the parties. If an agreement is left out, it is assumed not to exist. An agreement that is included is assumed to exist and is generally enforceable. If a written agreement contains mistakes, it is probably not valid or enforceable. For these reasons, it is extremely important for a listing agreement to be accurate, error-free, and complete.

Exclusive right-to-sell clauses

Generally, a written listing agreement requires as a minimum:

- names of all owners
- address or legal description of the listed property
- listing price
- expiration date
- commission terms
- authority granted

The following clause descriptions are found in a typical exclusive right-to-sell listing agreement.

Parties and authorization. The agreement should name all legal owners of the property, or duly authorized representatives of the owners, as the client party. It must also name the broker.

Real Property. It is critical to identify both the real property and any personal property that are for sale and included in the listing price.

Fixtures. Typical agreements list what fixtures are included in the sale specifically, and "all other things attached or affixed to the property" generally. The seller must then enter which items are excluded from the sale.

Personal Property. The listing agreement should include all personal property that is to be included in the transaction and listing price.

Listing price. A clause usually sets forth the gross price for the property and possibly the financing terms the owner will accept, particularly if seller financing or assumption of the seller's loan is involved.

The listing price is the seller's asking price for the property. This may or may not be the price the seller ultimately accepts. The full listing price does not have to be obtained for the broker to earn a commission. The listing price clause may also state the seller's agreement to pay customary closing costs.

Listing term. Exclusive listings must have a specific beginning and ending date of the listing agreement. Any provision for renewal of the listing term should be very specific.

To protect the broker, some listings contain a provision to extend the listing period in the event an expiration occurs during the period in which a sale contract is pending.

Agent's duties. This clause specifies the broker's responsibilities and authorization to carry out certain activities. These typically include marketing activities, multiple listing service activities, property access and showings, authority to allow other parties access, permission to inspect existing mortgage financing documents, and authority to accept deposits. Commonly, the clause specifically bars the broker from executing any contract on behalf of the owner.

Agent's compensation. A clause will identify the broker's fee and the necessary conditions for the fee to be earned. For instance, it may state that a commission is earned if a buyer is procured, a contract is executed, or the seller voluntarily transfers the property for any price during the listing period.

A fee clause usually provides for remedies in the event of default by the buyer or seller. In effect, if the seller breaches the listing without grounds after a buyer has been procured, the commission is payable. If the owner cannot sell the property for reasons beyond the owner's control, the owner is not liable for a commission. If the buyer breaches a sale contract, the owner and broker may split the buyer's earnest money deposit as liquidated damages, depending on state law.

Protection period. Many listings include a protection clause stating that, for a certain period after expiration, the owner is liable for the commission if the property sells to a party that the broker procured, unless the seller has since listed the property with another broker.

Multiple listing. This provision obtains the seller's consent to placing the listing in a multiple listing service and authorization to disseminate information about the listing to members.

Cooperation with other agents. This clause requires the seller to agree or refuse to cooperate with subagents or buyer agents in selling the property, under what terms, and whether the seller agrees to compensate these parties. Recent agreements stipulate that subagents and buyer agents must disclose their relationships to the buyer upon initial contact and subsequently in writing. There may also be a warning to the seller not to disclose confidential information to a buyer broker insofar as this agent is required to disclose all relevant information to the buyer.

Non-discrimination. Most exclusive listings contain an affirmation that the agent will conduct all affairs in compliance with state and federal fair housing and nondiscrimination laws.

Dual agency. In the absence of disclosure and consent, dual agency represents a conflict of interest for the broker. A good agreement specifically asks the owner to consent to or refuse to allow the broker's representation of both parties.

If the clause states that the owner refuses to accept dual agency, the broker agrees not to show the property to any buyers the broker represents.

If the seller accepts dual agency, the broker may represent both parties under the restrictions set forth in the listing. The restrictions are generally to protect the confidentialities of either party, particularly those relating to price and terms. Additionally, the broker covenants to deal honestly and impartially with the parties.

Other disclosures by agent. In addition to agency, other disclosures might be included to cover any direct or indirect interest the broker has in the transaction and special compensation the broker might be receiving from other parties connected with the transaction.

Seller's representations and promises. In this clause, the owner represents that he or she in fact owns the property in the manner stated in the listing, and is legally capable of delivering fee simple, marketable title.

The clause may further require the owner to warrant that he or she

- is not represented by another party and will not list the property elsewhere during the listing period
- will not lease the property during the listing period without approval
- agrees to provide necessary information
- will refer all prospects directly to the broker without prior direct negotiation
- has reviewed a sample "Offer to Purchase and Sell" contract
- will make the property presentable and available for showing at reasonable times upon notice by agent.

Seller's property condition disclosure. Most current listing forms require the seller to disclose the condition of the property to prospective buyers. New laws in most states allow buyers to cancel a sale contract if they have not received the seller's property condition disclosure before closing or occupancy or other deadline. In addition, the listing may include among the seller's duties the requirement to complete and provide the agent with a Lead Paint Hazard addendum. A copy of the required notice to buyers may be attached to the listing agreement as part of the agreement.

Seller's title and deed. A provision usually requires the owner to promise to deliver good and marketable title, title insurance, and to convey the property using a general warranty deed to a buyer. Without this covenant, the broker has no assurance that a transaction will occur, and in turn that he or she will be paid for procuring a buyer.

Flood hazard insurance. This clause requires the seller to disclose whether he or she is required to or presently maintains flood insurance on the property.

Escrow authorization. The seller authorizes escrow officers to disburse earned commission funds to the broker upon the broker's instructions to do so.

Other listing provisions. An exclusive listing might also provide for:

> ➤ *mediation*: in the event of a dispute, the owner agrees to arbitrate differences before filing a lawsuit
> ➤ *attorney fees*: the losing party in a lawsuit must pay court costs and attorney fees
> ➤ *acknowledgment*: the owner acknowledges reading and understanding the agreement
> ➤ *entire agreement*: the listing cannot be changed without written agreement; the listing sets forth all agreements made
> ➤ *binding effect*: listing is binding and enforceable
> ➤ *saving clause*: if a portion of the agreement is invalid or unenforceable, the balance of the agreement remains valid as permitted by law

Signatures. All owners and the broker must sign the listing and indicate the date of signing.

Exclusive buyer agency clauses

The exclusive buyer agency agreement is very similar to the exclusive right-to-sell agreement, the only significant differences being the agent's objectives and the fact that the principal is the buyer instead of the seller. The notable exception is how the agent is paid, as previously discussed. The following clauses distinguish the buyer agency agreement from the exclusive right-to sell agreement.

Buyer's representation of exclusivity. Here the buyer affirms that he or she is not represented by another agent. In addition, the buyer acknowledges an understanding of the agency relationship.

Agent compensation. This clause sets forth how the agent is to be paid, whether by retainer or commission, who is to pay the commission, and what the buyer owes the agent in the event the seller does not participate in the agent's compensation. Second, the clause establishes the circumstances under which the agent has earned the commission. This includes finding a property during the agreement term or the buyer contracting to buy a property shown by the agent within a stipulated period of time following expiration. In addition, the clause provides that the agent will be paid in the event the buyer defaults on a sale contract.

Other buyers acknowledged. In this provision, the buyer acknowledges that the agent is working with other buyers who may be in competition for any property the buyer is shown by the agent.

Check Your Understanding Quiz:

Chapter 5: Nevada Agency and Brokerage Agreements

Carefully read each question and provide your best answer based on what you learned in this module. Then check your answers against the Answer Key which immediately follows the quiz questions.

1. Pursuant to Nevada statutory law the duty of confidentiality owed by a licensee expires

    a. never.
    b. one year after termination of the brokerage agreement.
    c. two years after termination of the brokerage agreement.
    d. one year after the client buys property.

2. What form is needed in Nevada for a licensee to act for more than one party to a transaction?

    a. Dual Agency Authorization
    b. No specific form is required.
    c. Consent to Act
    d. Multiple Representation Prohibition Form

3. The "Waiver" form signed by a seller and the seller's broker waives the broker's duty

    a. to exercise reasonable skill and care.
    b. of confidentiality to the seller.
    c. to present all offers to the seller.
    d. to disclose material facts concerning the transaction to the seller.

4. Which of the following is NOT recognized by Nevada agency law?

    a. Single agency
    b. Acting for more than one party to a transaction
    c. Assigned agency
    d. Transactional agency

5. In Nevada, the only duty owed by a real estate licensee to a client that can be waived is

    a. The duty of confidentiality
    b. The duty to present all offers.
    c. The duty to exercise reasonable skill and care.
    d. The duty to disclose material facts concerning the transaction.

6. A brokerage agreement is a contract between a

    a. broker and a client.
    b. salesperson and a client.
    c. buyer and a seller.
    d. broker and the Nevada Real Estate Division

7. The duties owed by a Nevada real estate licensee are governed primarily by

    a. common law.
    b. case law.
    c. Federal law.
    d. Nevada statutory law.

8. When a broker represents two buyers interested in the same property

    a. it creates an almost unavoidable conflict of interest.
    b. it does not create a conflict of interest.
    c. the broker must assign a separate salesperson to represent both buyers.
    d. the broker must refer one of the buyers to a different brokerage firm.

9. In an assigned agency

    a. salespeople agree who will represent whom.
    b. the clients determine which salespeople will act on their behalf.
    c. the Real Estate Division assigns separate salespeople to represent the buyer and the seller.
    d. the broker assigns separate salespeople to represent the buyer and the seller.

10. In an assigned agency a salesperson may

    a. never disclose confidential information.
    b. only disclose confidential information to the broker.
    c. only disclose confidential information with permission from the Real Estate Division.
    d. disclose confidential information if a salesperson thinks it's in the best interest of the client.

11. An "ethical wall" is used in

    a. single agency.
    b. acting for more than one party to the transaction.
    c. assigned agency.
    d. open listings to determine procuring cause.

12. A duty of confidentiality is owed by a Nevada real estate licensee to

    a. the client.
    b. all parties in the transaction.
    c. any party with whom the licensee is a confidentiality agreement.
    d. the parties to a purchase contract.

13. Which of the following is NOT a duty owed by a licensee to client?

    a. A duty to disclose material facts concerning the transaction.
    b. A duty to present all offers made by and to the client.
    c. A duty to advise the client to seek advice from an expert regarding matters beyond the licensee's expertise.
    d. A duty to conduct an investigation of the property's condition as it relates to the transaction.

14. When a seller has waived the listing broker's duty to present all offers, a buyer's agent needs written permission from the listing broker to present an offer. This permission can be obtained through a form called

    a. Permission to Present Offer.
    b. Permission to Negotiate.
    c. Authorization to Negotiate Directly with Seller.
    d. Permission to Present and Negotiate Offer.

15. The Duties Owed by a Nevada Real Estate Licensee form must be presented

    a. as soon as is practicable.
    b. at first contact.
    c. after the party signs a brokerage agreement.
    d. after the party signs an offer.

16. Failure to include a definite termination date in a written brokerage agreement

    a. violates the statute of frauds.
    b. entitles the client to double damages in a lawsuit.
    c. entitles the client to treble (triple) damages in a lawsuit.
    d. allows the client to void the agreement and not pay the broker.

17. Which of the following is NOT real estate brokerage agreement?

    a. Exclusive Right to Sell
    b. Exclusive Agency Listing
    c. Property Management Agreement
    d. Open Buyer Brokerage Agreement

18. Which of the following statements is TRUE about Nevada real estate brokerage agreements?

    a. Nevada real estate brokerage agreements are NOT required to be in writing.
    b. Listing agreements are required to be in writing.
    c. Buyer representation agreements are required to be in writing.
    d. A listing agreement in excess of $250,000 must be in writing.

19. In which of the following brokerage agreements may a client hire several brokers?

    a. An open agency.
    b. An exclusive agency.
    c. An implied agency.
    d. An agency agreement without consideration agency.

20. In an open agency the broker receives compensation if the broker

    a. exercised reasonable skill and care to achieve the objectives of the brokerage agreement.
    b. found a buyer who meets the seller's terms.
    c. has followed all applicable laws and rules.
    d. gave the client reasonable advice.

21. Which of the following is NOT one of the requirements for an exclusive brokerage agreement?

    a. The agreement must be in writing.
    b. The agreement must be signed by all the parties.
    c. The agreement must have a definite termination date.
    d. The term of the agreement must not exceed one year.

22. Failure to include a definite termination date in an exclusive brokerage agreement may

    a. allow the client to recover treble (triple) damages.
    b. allow the client not to pay the broker.
    c. subject the broker to criminal liability.
    d. allow a court to rescind the purchase agreement.

23. Two buyer agents have a dispute regarding who was the procuring cause in transaction. The procuring cause is the agent who

    a. did the most work.
    b. set into motion an uninterrupted chain of events that led to the purchase.
    c. first showed the property to the buyer.
    d. first obtained the buyer as a client

24. What is the most commonly used listing agreement?

    a. Exclusive right to sell
    b. Exclusive agency listing
    c. Open listing
    d. Net listing

25. Who typically pays the buyer's broker?

    a. The listing broker from the commission earned
    b. The seller
    c. The buyer
    d. The lender

26. When a seller has waived the listing broker's duty to present all offers, a buyer's agent needs written permission from the listing broker to present an offer. This permission can be obtained through a form called

    a. Permission to Present Offer.
    b. Permission to Negotiate.
    c. Authorization to Negotiate Directly with Seller.
    d. Permission to Present and Negotiate Offer.

27. The protection clause found in many listing agreements

    a. protects the broker from lawsuits.
    b. allows the broker, in some circumstance, to obtain compensation even though the listing agreement has expired.
    c. protects the broker from misrepresentations made by the seller.
    d. waives the fee owed if the broker has not adequately protected the seller's interests.

Answer Key:

Chapter 5: Nevada Agency and Brokerage Agreements

1. b. one year after termination of the brokerage agreement.

2. c. Consent to Act

3. c. to present all offers to the seller.

4. d. Transactional agency

5. b. The duty to present all offers.

6. a. broker and a client.

7. d. Nevada statutory law.

8. a. it creates an almost unavoidable conflict of interest.

9. d. the broker assigns separate salespeople to represent the buyer and the seller.

10. b. only disclose confidential information to the broker.

11. c. assigned agency.

12. a. a client.

13. d. A duty to conduct an investigation of the property's condition as it relates to the transaction.

14. c. Authorization to Negotiate Directly with Seller.

15. a. as soon as practicable.

16. d. allows the client to void the agreement and not pay the broker.

17. c. Property Management Agreement

18. a. Nevada real estate brokerage agreements are NOT required to be in writing.

19. a. An open agency.

20. b. found a buyer who meets the seller's terms.

21. d. The term of the agreement must not exceed one year.

22. b. allow the client not to pay the broker.

23. b. set into motion an uninterrupted chain of events that led to the purchase.

24. a. Exclusive right to sell.

25. a. The listing broker from the commission earned

26. c. Authorization to Negotiate Directly with Seller.

27. b. allows the broker, in some circumstance, to obtain compensation even though the listing agreement has expired.

Chapter 6:
Broker–Salesperson Relationship

Legal relationships

Only a broker with an active broker's license can hire and employ a licensed salesperson. A licensed salesperson may work only for the employing broker and may not work for or receive direct compensation from any other broker.

Agent's scope of authority. Nevada real estate license laws provide for two distinct licenses to conduct real estate brokerage: the broker license and the salesperson license.

A licensed real estate broker is duly authorized to represent clients directly in brokering real estate. A sales agent, on the other hand, is only authorized to represent a broker and carry out such duties as the broker may legitimately delegate. In other words, a sales agent does not directly represent the client in a transaction but is rather the agent of the broker and subagent of the client. A sales agent is therefore a fiduciary of the employing broker.

As agent of a broker, a salesperson may offer properties for sale or lease, procure buyers, negotiate transaction terms, and otherwise conduct the business of brokerage. The agent, however, must act entirely on the broker's behalf.

A salesperson *may not*:

- ▶ bind a client to any contract
- ▶ receive compensation directly from a client
- ▶ accept a listing or deposit that is not in the name of the broker

Salesperson's employment status

A salesperson may be an independent contractor (IC) or an employee. In either case, the broker is responsible and liable for the sales agent's actions. Brokers are subject to guidelines of the U.S. Equal Employment Opportunity Commission (EEOC), a federal agency that enforces laws against workplace discrimination.

Independent contractor / broker relationship. Generally, a broker has limited control over the actions of a contractor. Specifically:

- ▶ a broker can require performance results, but is limited in demanding *how* a contractor performs the work. For example, a broker may not prescribe selling methods, meeting attendance, or office hours.

- ▶ an IC is responsible for income and social security taxes; the broker does not withhold taxes

- ▶ a broker cannot provide an IC with employee benefits such as health insurance or pension plans

Employee / broker relationship. A broker has greater control over the actions of an employee. Specifically:

> ► a broker can impose a sales methodology. In addition, a broker can enforce all office policies, including hours, meeting attendance, and telephone coverage.

> ► a broker must withhold income taxes and pay unemployment compensation tax on behalf of an employee

> ► an employee may receive the benefits enjoyed by the broker's non-selling employees

A written agreement between broker and employee or independent contractor should clearly state each party's duties and responsibilities to the other. In addition, the agreement should clarify the agent's compensation program as well as who is to pay for incidental business expenses.

Real estate assistant or personal assistant. Brokers and salespersons may hire licensed or unlicensed employees to assist them with a variety of tasks. Unlicensed assistants may perform clerical or ministerial acts, but nothing requiring a license. Licensed assistants may perform tasks requiring a license. Unlicensed assistants usually may be compensated directly by the sales associate they work for, but licensed assistants must be compensated by the employing broker and are subject to that broker's supervision.

Obligations and responsibilities

Sales agent's duties and responsibilities. In accepting employment from a broker, a salesperson generally makes a commitment to:

> ► work diligently to sell the broker's listings
> ► work diligently to procure new listings
> ► promote the business reputation of the broker
> ► abide by the broker's established policies
> ► fulfill the fiduciary duties owed clients as their subagent
> ► maintain insurance policies as required by the broker
> ► have transportation for conducting business, as required by the broker
> ► conform to ethical standards imposed by broker and trade organization
> ► uphold all covenants and provisions of the employment agreement

Broker's obligations to the sales agent. In employing a salesperson, a broker generally makes a commitment to:

> ► make the brokerage's listings available
> ► make the brokerage's market and property data available
> ► provide whatever training was promised at the time of hiring
> ► provide whatever office support was promised at the time of hiring
> ► uphold the commission structure and expense reimbursement policy
> ► conform to ethical standards imposed by the broker's trade organization
> ► uphold all covenants and provisions of the employment agreement

BROKER SUPERVISION OF LICENSEE

Broker liability   Only brokers may act independently. All other licensees must act on behalf of a broker and under the supervision of a broker.

The broker is tasked with supervising the associated licensees and employees' activities and the operation of the broker's business. Supervision is required for independent contractors and employees alike. Consequently, while the licensee is liable for his or her own conduct, the supervising broker is also vicariously liable for the licensee's conduct.

Supervisory duties   **Training.** The broker is tasked by Nevada law with teaching associated licensees the fundamentals of real estate and the ethics of the profession.

Policies and procedures. Nevada law also tasks the broker with establishing policies, rules, procedures, and systems that allow the broker to review and manage the following without limitation:

> - all real estate transactions performed by an associated licensee
> - all documents that may have a material impact on the rights of a party to the transaction
> - filing, storing, and maintaining related documents
> - handling of all money received on behalf of the broker
> - advertising any service that requires a real estate license
> - licensee familiarity with federal and state laws that govern real estate transactions, including prohibitions against discrimination

Broker-salesperson assistant. In meeting the requirement to review and manage the licensees' activities, the broker is to consider how many licensees are associated with the broker, how many individuals are employed by the broker, and how many branch offices are operated by the broker. The broker may use an associated broker-salesperson to assist in monitoring compliance with these requirements as long as the broker does not relinquish overall supervision of the licensees. The broker may not use a salesperson for this assistance.

Employment contracts. The broker may also enter into contracts with associated licensees agreeing that the licensees are employed as independent contractors. The contract must include material aspects of the broker-licensee relationship, including supervision, and must be signed and dated by both the broker and the licensee.

LICENSEE RESPONSIBILITIES

Licensees need a Nevada real estate license prior to performing any activities that require licensure and involve compensation. The licensee must be associated with a broker or employed by an owner-developer. The licensee may only work on behalf of the broker or owner-developer and under the supervision of that broker or owner-developer.

Association with broker

Licensees associated with a broker have the following responsibilities:

> ➢ may accept compensation, referral fees, bonuses, or gifts only through the associated broker; if the licensee has changed broker association and is still owed compensation from the previous broker, the licensee may accept that compensation
> ➢ must turn over to the associated broker any money or other compensation received from a third party within one business day of receipt of the funds
> ➢ must not pay referral fees or commissions to other licensees or to unlicensed individuals
> ➢ must disclose to all parties to a transaction any personal interest in an escrow business or company prior to depositing any money received into an account in that company or business
> ➢ must not participate in naming a false consideration in any document regardless of disclosure or seller agreement
> ➢ must provide copies of executed contracts or offers to the appropriate parties within a reasonable time and to their broker within 5 calendar days
> ➢ must cooperate completely and honestly with the Division and any of its requests
> ➢ must keep each brokerage agreement to be reviewed and audited by the Division
> ➢ must comply with statutory laws over common laws; if a common law conflicts with the requirements of a Nevada statute, the statute takes precedence over the common law

Office policy manual

Nevada laws and regulations do not require a broker to have a written office policy manual. However, it is difficult to imagine how a real estate broker could comply with supervisorial duties without having a written manual. The National Association of REALTORS® states that an office manual should do the following:

> ➢ Provide a clear understanding of the relationship between broker and sales associates, management and employees, and administrative functions and sales functions.
> ➢ Permit the anticipation of and resolution of controversies before they arise.
> ➢ Stabilize both management and sales by building confidence that both management and sales associates know the rules by which the game is to be played.
> ➢ Forbid favoritism, since all must operate within the framework of the manual's predetermined rules and guidelines.
> ➢ Provide stability of organization and permit the staff to function effectively in the absence of management

To comply with supervisory the following topics that should be covered:

- ▶ Independent Contactor/Employment Agreement
- ▶ Sales Meetings
- ▶ Functions of Unlicensed Office Personnel
- ▶ Teams
- ▶ Cooperation and Compensation Policy
- ▶ Agency Disclosure Policy
- ▶ Listing Procedures
- ▶ Buyer Representation Procedures
- ▶ Social Media Policy

Standard forms. Standard forms save time and protect against the unauthorized practice of law. Since they are most often prepared by lawyers familiar with the market area, they can address contingencies that are common in the area in a manner that reflects the real estate laws of the state. On the other hand, a licensee often needs to adapt a standardized form for a client by assisting with filling in blanks, modifying terms, and attaching addenda. The licensee must always remain aware of the limitations the state has placed on such activities.

Here are a few of the standard forms a brokerage should provide for its agents and affiliates:

- ▶ buyer and seller representation agreements, exclusive and non-exclusive
- ▶ agreement to show property
- ▶ purchase and sale agreement
- ▶ agency disclosure form
- ▶ property condition disclosure, disclaimer, and exemption form
- ▶ lease agreement
- ▶ personal interest disclosure form
- ▶ referral for service disclosure form
- ▶ lead-based paint disclosure form
- ▶ special disclosure forms (mold, radon, subsurface sewage system, impact fees/adequate facilities taxes, etc.)
- ▶ referral agreement
- ▶ independent contractor agreement
- ▶ closing checklist

COMMISSIONS AND OTHER COMPENSATION

Definition of commission

Nevada law defines commission as any fee or other compensation agreed upon by a broker and a client which is specified in the brokerage agreement. Before a licensee can accept compensation or legally prove he or she is owed compensation, the licensee must be a licensed broker who has entered into a brokerage agreement with the client. The brokerage agreement will include provisions for the rate and source of compensation or commission.

Sources of compensation

The source of compensation will be either from the client or from a third party. The client-source is typically a seller. The third-party source can be a listing broker paying a buyer's broker or a listing broker paying a cooperating broker when an MLS is involved. Another third-party source is one broker paying referral fees to another broker.

Commission rates

The rate is typically a percentage of the property's sale price, negotiable between the broker and client or between the broker and a cooperating broker. Rates may also be paid as flat fees, net listings, or fee-for-service arrangements. Net listings include a set sale price by the seller with any amount received over that price being the broker's compensation. While net listings are prohibited in many states, they are allowed in Nevada. However, many multiple listing services still refuse them because the cooperating broker's commission cannot be reasonably determined.

Quantum meruit is another means of determining the compensation rate. It is used by the courts when there is no express agreement or when the agreement fails. The court then looks at established customs to determine the commission the broker should be paid for his or her services. Quantum meruit cannot be used with faulty exclusive brokerage agreements.

The Real Estate Settlement Procedures Act and Anti-trust laws also have an impact on determining compensation. In addition to federal laws, Nevada has its own anti-trust law. As with the federal law, Nevada's law makes price fixing, territory dividing between competitors, customer allocating, or area monopolizing illegal.

Who may pay or receive

A salesperson or broker-salesperson can negotiate the compensation rate on behalf of the broker. However, a salesperson or a broker-salesperson may not directly pay another licensee or cooperating broker. Compensation must be paid by the broker him or herself.

Licensees may only be compensated by the associated broker or the employing owner-developer. Consequently, compensation between a broker or owner-developer and an associated licensee is negotiated between those two individuals. There is no compensation rate mandated by law for either licensees or brokers and owner-developers.

The law does mandate, however, that no compensation may be paid or offered directly or indirectly to an unlicensed person for any activities or services that require licensure, including referral and finder's fees. A broker may compensate or pay a commission to a broker licensed in another state.

Right to compensation

When a broker lists a property for sale, he or she earns compensation, or a commission, by securing a buyer pursuant to the provisions of the listing agreement. The buyer must be ready, willing, and financially able to purchase the property at the seller's listing price or negotiated price. In some purchase agreements, the broker is to receive compensation even if the buyer defaults on the deal, with the buyer sometimes being the party who is liable for paying the seller for any commission already paid to the broker.

Payment of compensation is due to the broker when the terms of the brokerage agreement have been fulfilled. In certain agreements, the commission is due to the broker when he or she finds a buyer pursuant to the terms of the agreement. In others, the commission is due at escrow closing. If the transaction is for a service not related to a property sale, the compensation is due after the service is provided. Consequently, it is important that the compensation terms of the agreement be very clear.

Unless otherwise stated in the brokerage agreement, a seller must also pay a broker if the seller accepts a purchase price lower than the listed price. The seller is not allowed to refuse an offer to purchase and then wait until the brokerage agreement has expired to change his or her mind to accept the same offer, all to avoid paying the broker's commission.

Disclosure

Because brokers are required to disclose in writing the source of any compensation the broker expects to receive, a broker who expects to receive compensation from more than one party to a transaction must obtain the consent of each party to do so. The broker needs only to disclose the source of compensation and not the amount.

Check Your Understanding Quiz:

Chapter 6: Broker-Salesperson Relationship

Carefully read each question and provide your best answer based on what you learned in this module. Then check your answers against the Answer Key which immediately follows the quiz questions.

1. Pursuant to Nevada law, a licensed real estate salesperson may be hired to operate in a brokerage by

    a. any other real estate licensee.
    b. only a licensed real estate broker.
    c. only a licensed real estate broker or licensed broker-salesperson
    d. any real estate licensee if approved by the Real Estate Division.

2. A licensed real estate salesperson acts directly on behalf of

    a. the broker.
    b. the client.
    c. the Real Estate Division.
    d. Any unrepresented party to the transaction.

3. A real estate salesperson generally receives a

    a. salary.
    b. hourly wage.
    c. split of the broker's commission.
    d. combination of salary in hourly wage.

4. Marilyn, a real estate salesperson, did an outstanding job for her clients. Now they want to give Marilyn a $500 bonus. May Marilyn legally accept the bonus?

    a. Yes, she did the outstanding job.
    b. Yes, but it must be paid to Marilyn's broker first and the broker can pay her.
    c. No, when extra money is received it is presumed that something illegal happened.
    d. No, compensation cannot exceed the amount specified in the brokerage agreement.

5. Who can act independently of any other party in Nevada?

    a. A broker-salesperson
    b. A salesperson with at least 10 years' experience
    c. A broker
    d. A broker who has posted a bond with the Real Estate Commission

6. The fee typically paid to a listing real estate broker in a purchase transaction is

    a. a flat fee expressed as a dollar amount.
    b. the difference between a specified amount for the seller and the actual net proceeds.
    c. a percentage of the purchase price.
    d. a fee for services arrangement.

7. Most real estate salespersons are retained as

    a. independent contractors earning hourly wage.
    b. independent contractors earning a commission.
    c. employees earning a salary.
    d. employees earning an hourly wage.

8. The core activity of real estate brokerage is the business of

    a. listing property for sale.
    b. representing clients who want to buy property.
    c. finding people to rent property.
    d. procuring a buyer, seller, tenant, or property on behalf of a client for the purpose of completing a transaction.

Answer Key:

Chapter 6: Broker-Salesperson Relationship

1. b. only a licensed real estate broker.

2. a. the broker.

3. c. split of the broker's commission.

4. b. Yes, but it must be paid to Marilyn's broker first and the broker can pay her.

5. c. A broker

6. c. a percentage of the purchase price.

7. b. independent contractors earning a commission.

8. d. procuring a buyer, seller, tenant, or property on behalf of a client for the purpose of completing a transaction.

Chapter 7:
Risk Management

Risk is the chance of losing something. Its two dimensions are the probability of occurrence and the extent of exposure to monetary or non-monetary consequences. Since most risks are related to judgments and decisions, the real estate licensee, who makes numerous complex decisions every day, faces a high degree of risk potential.

Risk management is a structured approach to dealing with the uncertainties and consequences of risk. In real estate practice, the aim is to reduce risk to an acceptable level through anticipation and planning.

RISK MANAGEMENT STRATEGIES

Four well-established strategies for managing risk are:

- ▶ Avoidance (elimination)
- ▶ Reduction (mitigation, sharing)
- ▶ Transference (outsourcing, insuring)
- ▶ Retention (acceptance and budgeting)

Not all of these strategies are always possible or available, but a real estate firm or licensee who fails to make a conscious effort to employ one or more of them increases the likelihood of loss from the many potential risks that are always present in the real estate business.

Avoidance

Avoidance involves refraining from an activity that carries risk. One can avoid the risks of being in an automobile accident by not riding in automobiles. Avoiding risks also means missing the opportunity to benefit from the avoided activity. By avoiding automobile travel, one is confined to modes of transportation, such as buses and walking, that do not offer the same high degree of personal freedom and efficiency. Complete avoidance of risk in real estate practice is almost impossible. A broker, for instance, may believe that hiring only experienced affiliates eliminates the risk that affiliates will commit license law violations. However, even experienced practitioners may not know the law, and, sometimes, people break the law deliberately. The risk may be reduced, but it remains.

Reduction

Reduction involves taking steps to reduce the probability or the severity of a potential loss. However, this strategy may result in reducing risk in one area only to increase it in another. A familiar example is a sprinkler system that dispenses water to reduce the risk of fire but at the same time increases the risk of water damage.

In real estate practice, one risk reduction tactic is to share responsibility for making a decision. The agent provides the consumer with expertise, and perhaps some advice, but lets the consumer decide how much to offer. In this way, the agent gets some relief from the risks inherent in the buyer's decision to purchase.

Transference

Transference means passing the risk to another party, by contract or other means. An insurance policy is the common example, but sometimes the wording of a sales or personal services contract can transfer risk without resorting to insurance.

In the real estate business, transference is typically and most successfully accomplished by means of an errors and omissions (E&O) insurance policy, either on the individuals in a firm or on the firm itself. State law may require such insurance.

Retention

Retention of risk means entering into an activity in spite of known risks and taking full responsibility for the consequences. This is, in effect, self-insurance, the only strategy left when risk cannot be reduced or transferred and one has decided not to avoid it because of the desirability of the potential benefits.

RISK MANAGEMENT PROCEDURES

Experience shows that the most practical strategies for risk management in real estate practice are reduction and transference, with procedures focusing on:

- ▶ Education
- ▶ Disclosure
- ▶ Documentation
- ▶ Insurance

Education

Education is the first line of defense against risk. When agents are familiar with the forms provided by the office, how and when to complete them and where to send them, the likelihood of errors is reduced. Likewise, agents need to be able to identify and understand common contract elements, complete contract forms developed by attorneys, and evaluate offers received from co-op agents on their listings without committing a license violation or breach of law.

In most states, brokers have a legal obligation to provide training to affiliated licensees. Licensees also have the obligation to seek out appropriate education and training outside the brokerage to ensure that they know how to comply with the law. In addition, licensees must satisfy legal requirements for continuing education, while those who care about personal excellence will seek further education and training to enhance their professional skills.

Disclosure

By ensuring that all parties have the information they are entitled to, proper disclosure reduces the risk that clients and customers will accuse a licensee of misleading or inducing them to make a decision with incomplete information. Further, laws in every state require disclosures of one kind or another.

Disclosure may be made in writing or verbally and may or may not require written acknowledgment from the receiving party.

Required disclosures usually include:

- ▶ agency relationships
- ▶ property condition
- ▶ duties and obligations
- ▶ personal interest in the transaction
- ▶ personal interest in referrals

Documentation and Record keeping

Documentation provides evidence of compliance with laws and regulations. It proves what clients and customers and licensees said and did in a transaction. Some documentation is required by law.

The components of a thoroughly documented paper trail include:

- ▶ Policy and procedure manuals
- ▶ Standard forms
- ▶ Communication records
- ▶ Transaction records
- ▶ Contracts
- ▶ Accounting
- ▶ Other important documents

Policy manual. A written and uniformly enforced company policy lets everyone in the firm know what to expect before problems arise. The policy manual should cover the company's rules in such areas as floor duty privileges, assignment of relocation properties to agents, referrals between agents within the company, and requirements for continuing education, sales meeting participation, and property tours.

A company policy and procedures manual should also spell out how to handle handling consumers' funds and documents, conducting consumer transactions, dealing with MLS-related matters, placing signage, and to all compliance-related procedures prescribed by state or federal law, for example, license, banking and fair housing laws. Adherence to the manual reduces the risk that an individual will inadvertently commit an unlawful act. Whenever changes are made to the policy or procedures manual, each agent should sign the revised manual as evidence that the agent has examined it.

Standard forms. Standard forms save time and protect against the unauthorized practice of law. Since they are most often prepared by lawyers familiar with the market area, they can address contingencies that are common in the area in a manner that reflects the real estate laws of the state. On the other hand, a licensee often needs to adapt a standardized form for a client by assisting with filling in blanks, modifying terms, and attaching addenda. The licensee must always remain aware of the limitations the state has placed on such activities.

Here are a few of the standard forms a brokerage should provide for its agents and affiliates:

- buyer and seller representation agreements, exclusive and non-exclusive
- agreement to show property
- purchase and sale agreement
- agency disclosure form
- property condition disclosure, disclaimer, and exemption form
- lease agreement
- personal interest disclosure form
- referral for service disclosure form
- lead-based paint disclosure form
- special disclosure forms (mold, radon, subsurface sewage system, impact fees/adequate facilities taxes, etc.)
- referral agreement
- independent contractor agreement
- closing checklist

Communication records. Some communications with transaction parties are good and necessary for business. Others are required by law, such as certain disclosures. A transaction checklist is a good tool for managing risk associated with the failure to make required communications to all principals and for keeping track of required communications from co-op agents.

Retaining evidence that information has been communicated is a necessary procedure. Electronic communications should be archived on suitable electronic media. Copies of mailed or faxed communications should be maintained in the transaction folder.

It is always difficult to document telephone or face-to-face conversations, especially with the constant use of cell phones from a variety of locations. It is a good practice to make brief notes at the time and then write them up later for mailing or faxing to the other party. Be sure, however, that you can produce these notes on demand, lest you be accused later of withholding documentation that has been promised.

Maintaining a good record of communications is useful for resolving disagreements where parties dispute what has been said because it allows the agent to produce a dated document that resolves the issue definitively.

Transaction records. State laws require licensees to document transactions. Firms are required to keep written records of all real estate transactions for a number of years (usually three to five) after closing or termination. Required records typically include:

- listing agreements
- offers
- contracts
- closing statements
- agency agreements
- disclosure documents
- correspondence and other communication records
- notes and any other relevant information

Accounting. In addition to other accounting records, there is the requirement to maintain written accounting of escrow funds. For each transaction, property, and principal, escrow records will include:

- depositor
- date of deposit
- date of withdrawal
- payee
- other information deemed pertinent by the real estate commission

Other documents. Additional documents may be required by law or regulation, or should be kept simply as protection in case of disputes and lawsuits. These would include copies of advertising materials, materials used in training agents, records of compliance with continuing education requirements, safety manuals, and anything else that shows how the firm conducts its business and safeguards its staff as well as the rights of consumers.

Insurance

Many forms of insurance are available for property owners and managers. Some of these types are also used to manage certain risks of brokers and licensees.

General Liability. General liability insurance provides coverage for risks incurred by a property owner when the public or a licensee enters the owned property (**public liability**). The insurer pays the covered claim and legal fees, costs, and expenses, including medical expenses, resulting from owner negligence or other causes. This type of insurance does not cover **professional liability,** for which an Errors & Omissions policy is necessary.

Errors and Omissions. Professional liability is of two general types:

1. Unprofessional conduct – a claim that one has failed to carry out fiduciary duties and provide an acceptable standard of care

2. Breach of contract – a claim that one has failed to perform services under the terms of a contract in a timely manner

The primary method for transferring the professional liability risks of brokers, managers, and licensees is Errors & Omissions (E&O) insurance. A standard E&O policy provides coverage for "damages resulting from any negligent act, error or omission arising out of Professional Services." A standard policy does NOT cover:

- violations of law
- fraudulent, dishonest, criminal or malicious acts
- mishandling of escrow moneys, earnest money deposits, or security deposits
- antitrust violations
- sexual harassment
- Fair Housing violations
- agent-owned properties
- environmental violations
- failure to detect or disclose environmental conditions, including mold

▸ acts committed prior to licensure or after termination of active status

▸ activities as an appraiser if licensing other than a real estate license is required

E&O insurance, in short, covers "mistakes" but not crimes.

Fire and hazard. The risks of property damage caused by fire, wind, hail, smoke, civil disturbance, and other such causes are covered by fire and hazard insurance.

Flood. The risks of property damage caused by floods, heavy rains, snow, drainage failures, and failed public infrastructures such as dams and levies are covered by a specialized flood policy. Regular hazard policies do not include flood coverage.

Other insurance. Other common types of insurance coverage for income and commercial properties include:

▸ **casualty**—coverage for specific risks, such as theft, vandalism, burglary, illness and accident, machinery damage

▸ **workers' compensation**—hospital and medical coverage for employees injured in the course of employment, mandated by state laws

▸ **contents and personal property**—coverage for building contents and personal property when they are not actually on the building premises

▸ **consequential loss, use, and occupancy**—coverage for the business losses resulting from a disaster, such as loss of rent and other revenue, when the property cannot be used for business

▸ **surety bond**—coverage against losses resulting from criminal or negligent acts of an employee

PRIMARY AREAS OF RISK

Risks for licensees are present every day in business transactions. Many of these risks carry legal implications as well as possible financial and professional consequences.

Agency

The risks of agency will occur in one of two areas:

▸ the requirement to inform and disclose
▸ the requirement to carry out an agency duty.

Most states require agency relationships to be in writing and to be disclosed to all parties to a transaction. State law may spell out agency duties, or the duties may be a part of general agency law. In states that do not use agency, there is still the obligation to explain and disclose the nature of the relationship.

Disclosure requirements. A licensee may be acting in a transaction as facilitator, agent, subagent, designated agent, single agent, dual agent, non-agent or in some capacity. Regardless of status, the licensee must follow state disclosure requirements. These are, typically, to:

- ▶ disclose status *verbally* to other licensees on initial contact
- ▶ disclose status *verbally* to buyer and seller before providing real estate services
- ▶ confirm the disclosure *in writing* before signing a listing agreement or presenting a purchase offer (to an unrepresented seller) or before preparing a purchase offer (to an unrepresented buyer)
- ▶ get a *signed receipt* indicating the written disclosure has been made

Carrying out the duties of agency also require disclosures of :

- ▶ personal interest the agent has in a transaction (such as owner or buyer)
- ▶ personal benefit the agent will derive from a service referral
- ▶ required property and market information
- ▶ information about customers a client is entitled to have

Duties. A licensee who acts for a principal in a real estate transaction is required by law to assume certain responsibilities toward the parties to the transaction. Whether a state applies the fiduciary duties of agency law or specifies its own duties toward clients and consumers, the basic duties remain:

To all parties
- ▶ honesty
- ▶ fairness
- ▶ reasonable care and skill
- ▶ disclosures

To clients
- ▶ skill
- ▶ care
- ▶ diligence
- ▶ loyalty
- ▶ obedience
- ▶ confidentiality
- ▶ accounting
- ▶ full disclosure

The duty to exercise **skill, care and diligence** means that licensees may not be casual or negligent in their actions. Licensee negligence is actionable when principals are harmed by the licensee's failure.

The duty of **loyalty** requires the agent to *put the client's interests above those of everyone else*, including his or her own.

The duty of **obedience** requires the agent to act on the principal's wishes regarding the transaction as long as they do not result in any illegal action. The duty of obedience never overrides the legal obligation of agents to deal fairly and honestly with all parties.

The duty of **confidentiality** requires the agent to hold in confidence any information that would harm the client's interests or bargaining position or anything else the client wishes to keep secret, unless the law requires disclosure. The duty of confidentiality survives the termination of the listing contract.

The duty of **accounting** applies to all funds involved in a real estate transaction. Accounts must be maintained as required by law, and escrow funds are to be handled strictly in accordance with the law.

The duty of **disclosure** applies to both parties to a transaction, although usually with some differences. Proper disclosure to customers primarily concerns agency, property condition, and environmental hazards. To the client, it generally concerns all known facts regarding the property and the transaction, including information about the other transaction party. State laws prescribe what may, must, and must not be disclosed. Licensees must be vigilant to avoid oversights and conflicts of interest that can lead to a disclosure to the wrong party or disclosure of information that is confidential.

Conflicts of interest. Conflicts of interest arise when an agent forgets to put the best interests of a client ahead of those of everyone else. This can happen in situations involving undisclosed dual agencies, broker-owned listings, licensees buying for their own account, vendor referrals, and property management subcontracting of services, among many others. Even ordinary, everyday transactions carry a built-in risk of conflict of interest. Consider the fact that a licensee usually receives no compensation for a failed transaction. Therefore, it is in the licensee's interest to see the transaction completed, even if it may not be in the client's best interest. A negative result from a home inspection or other test has the potential to cause a buyer to back out of a contract. A licensee who has forgotten whose best interest should be primary might be tempted to recommend inspectors who will overlook problems in exchange for receiving referrals. Licensees must always disclose any self-interest they have in a transaction, and always remember their duties to clients and consumers.

Confidentiality. Licensees have a responsibility to maintain the confidentiality of certain kinds of information they obtain concerning clients and customers. The duty to maintain confidentiality generally survives the termination of a listing agreement into perpetuity. If it seems that revealing confidential information might benefit the client, the licensee should obtain the client's written permission to proceed.

Confidential information generally includes information about a client's motivations in a transaction, financial and personal details, and information specifically designated as confidential by the client. Public information, such as that contained in public records, information that becomes known without the licensee's participation, or that the client reveals to another, is not considered confidential.

State laws often require businesses to provide security for the personal information they obtain about consumers. Security procedures should protect personal information from unauthorized access, destruction, use, modification, or disclosure. Confidential information, when it is not to be retained, must be disposed of in a secure manner.

Penalties. Possible penalties for breach of agency relationships include:

- ▸ rescission of transaction
- ▸ loss of compensation
- ▸ fees and costs
- ▸ punitive damages
- ▸ ethics discipline
- ▸ license discipline

Property disclosures

Property condition. Most states (including Nevada) require the seller of a residential property to deliver to the buyer a written disclosure or disclaimer about the property's condition, including any material defects the owner knows about. The disclosure is usually required before any purchase contract is accepted.. A second disclosure may be required at closing. The licensee should always obtain the parties' signatures acknowledging receipt of these disclosures.

Depending on the state, the licensee may have no further duty to disclose property condition after properly informing parties of their rights and obligations. However, the licensee may still be subject to legal action for

- ▸ deliberately distorting the facts (intentional misrepresentation)
- ▸ cheating any party (fraud)
- ▸ concealing or failing to disclose adverse facts which the licensee knew about or should have known about (intentional or unintentional misrepresentation)

Lead-based paint and other disclosures. Federal law requires sellers of houses built before 1978 to make a lead-based paint disclosure before accepting an offer to purchase. The licensee must tell the seller about this requirement, give the seller the proper disclosure form, and make sure that the buyer receives it.

The licensee must also make sure the seller discloses any other circumstances the situation and the law require, which may include:

- ▸ wood infestation inspection report
- ▸ soil test report
- ▸ subsurface sewage disposal system permit disclosure
- ▸ impact fees or adequate facilities taxes disclosure
- ▸ mold and radon reports or treatments

Listing and selling process

Nature and accuracy of the listing agreement. In most states, a listing agreement is enforceable only if it is in writing. Most states forbid net listings, because they violate the requirement that a valid listing agreement must specify a selling price and the agent's compensation. The licensee, in accordance with the duty of due diligence, must verify the accuracy of the statements in the listing regarding the property, the owner, and the owner's representations. Especially important facts for a broker or agent to verify are:

- the property condition
- ownership status
- the client's authority to act

An agent who does not to act with a reasonable degree of due diligence in these matters may be exposed to liability if it turns out that the property is not as represented or the client cannot perform the contract as promised.

Comparative Market Analysis (CMA). In preparing a Comparative Market Analysis, licensees should guard against using the terms "appraisal" and "value," which are reserved for the use of certified appraisers. Misuse of these terms could lead to a charge of misrepresenting oneself as an appraiser. In discussing listed properties with clients or customers, real estate licensees should be careful to use guarded terms such as "recommended listing price," "recommended purchase price,' and "recommended listing price range."

Agents should make every effort to help the sellers find a reasonable listing price based on the current market. If the CMA leads the seller to list at a price that is too high, the seller may blame the agent when the transaction fails because of an appraisal that comes in below the selling price. To minimize this risk, it is best to be conservative in the CMA and retain documentation that the seller went above the recommended price in spite of the agent's advice.

Estimate of Closing Costs. In preparing an estimate of closing costs for a seller or buyer, there is the risk of forgetting something, leading to an unpleasant surprise when the consumer suddenly faces unexpected costs or conditions. Licensees should use their broker's form, if there is one, and make it clear to the consumer that it is only an estimate of likely costs, not a statement of actual costs. In some states, brokers and agents do not prepare closing cost estimates, leaving that task to the lender.

Advertising. State and federal laws regulate advertising, including the federal Fair Housing laws as they pertain to discriminatory advertising and providing of services. Advertising includes electronic communication, social media/networking, and internet marketing. Usage must be consistent with company image and legal requirements. The license laws of most states list illegal advertising actions subject to discipline such as:

- making any substantial and intentional misrepresentation
- making any promise that might cause a person to enter into a contract or agreement when the promise is one the licensee cannot or will not abide by
- making continued and blatant misrepresentations or false promises through affiliate brokers, other persons, or any advertising medium
- making misleading or untruthful statements in any advertising, including using the term "Realtor" when not authorized to do so

and using any other trade name, insignia or membership in a real estate organization when the licensee is not a member.

Committing such acts may result in license suspension or revocation.

Authorizations and Permissions. Licensees should stay within the bounds of the authority granted by the agency agreement or must not do anything requiring permission without first getting that permission in writing. For instance, permission should be obtained before doing any of the following unless the listing agreement specifically grants the authority:

- post a sign on the property
- remove other signs
- show the property
- hand out the property condition disclosure
- distribute marketing materials
- advertise in various media
- use a multiple listing service
- cooperate with other licensees
- divide the commission or negotiate a commission split
- share final sales data with the MLS
- place a lock box on the property
- appoint subagents
- appoint a designated agent
- change agency status

Scope of expertise. Real estate licensees are not, by nature, financial consultants, accountants, appraisers, soil scientists, well diggers, lawyers, decorators, contractors, builders, plumbers, carpenters, inspectors, prognosticators, and a number of other kinds of expert. However, in today's competitive environment, consumers often demand much more from a licensee than the traditional basic services. An agent who fails to live up to prevailing standards may be held liable for negligence, fraud, or violation of state real estate license laws and regulations. At the same time, agents must be particularly careful about the temptation to misrepresent themselves as experts and offer inappropriate expert advice. Disclaimer and referral are always the best risk control procedures to forestall an accusation of misrepresentation from a consumer who claims to have been harmed by reliance on the licensee's non-existent expertise. The exact nature of the services to be provided should be stated as clearly as possible in the listing agreement.

Contracting process

According to the Statute of Frauds, all contacts for real estate must be in writing to be enforceable. Contracts that contain incorrect information or are inadequately prepared can pose a serious liability for a licensee. To avoid such a situation, it is imperative for the contract to reflect the terms that the parties have agreed upon in the most accurate and honest manner. The agent must also be careful to comply with the letter of the real estate law. Violations can jeopardize the enforceability of a listing or sales contract, in addition to resulting in criminal prosecution.

Common risks and errors in the contracting process include:

> ▶ using an illegal form
>
> A licensee may be punished for using any real estate listing agreement form, sales contract form, or offer to purchase form that lacks a *definite termination date*.

> ▶ failing to state inclusions and exclusions
>
> The parties should identify as included in or excluded from the transfer any ambiguous items. Unwritten agreements between the parties are a source of later dispute and trouble.

> ▶ failing to track the progress of contingency satisfaction
>
> The time period for completing contingencies such as inspections is specific and limited. Failure to meet or waive a condition may terminate the contract. A "time is of the essence" clause in the standard agreement makes the time period for contingencies critical.

> ▶ mistakes in entering data in a form
>
> All data should be checked and verified: dates, times, amounts, warranties, descriptions, names, representations, promises, procedures, authority, etc. One way to reduce risk in the contracting process is to use a checklist that covers all the contract items.

Unauthorized practice of law. The unintentional practice of law without a license is a great risk in the contracting process, as well as in the representation process. It is illegal for real estate professionals who are not attorneys to draw up contracts for transactions they are not involved in or to charge a separate fee for preparing a contract.

Such licensees may fill in blanks or make deletions on a preprinted contract form prepared by a lawyer. While a licensee may make deletions, additions to a form should be drafted by an attorney. The principals themselves can make changes as long as each change is signed or initialed by all signers. Preprinted riders can often be attached as addenda to a contract without an attorney.

It is also illegal for real estate licensees who are not lawyers to give legal advice or interpret contract language. Licensees, however, may express opinions. For instance, if a licensee believes that a party has grasped the meaning of a contract, it is permissible to say something like, "Though I am not an attorney, in my opinion your understanding of this contract is correct." It would be questionable to make a definitive statement like, "That's correct."

Fair Housing

The risk of violating fair housing laws can be minimized through ongoing education that addresses both the content and the intent of the laws. It is especially necessary for paperwork and documentation to be accurate and concise in a situation where a fair housing issue could arise.

Advertising. The Fair Housing Act forbids real estate advertising that mentions race, color, religion, national origin, sex, handicap, or familial status in any way that suggests preference or discrimination. State laws may add other protected categories, such as creed and age.

Risk can be reduced by the use of street names or other non-biased geographical references when stating where the property is located, and by describing the property rather than the type of persons who might live in or around it. Even if a home appears "ideal for a young family," it is best not to advertise it as such. Such advertising would exclude other groups such as singles, the elderly, and older families.

In advertising the sale or rental of housing covered by the Fair Housing Act, HUD recommends using the Fair Housing Logo or phrase "Equal Housing Opportunity."

Answering questions. When faced with questions that might lead to a *steering* charge or other violation of fair housing laws, it is best for the licensee to limit the response to features of the home and to the process of selling, buying, and listing properties, and refer the questioner to someone else to answer questions about such matters as the demographic make-up of the neighborhood. It is illegal for the licensee to voice an opinion based on race, religion, color, creed, national origin, sex, handicap, elderliness, or familial status. The agent should explain this fact to the buyer and be wary of any situation where the agent's behavior might be construed as discriminatory.

Listing agreements. Before entering into a listing agreement, a licensee should explain that it is necessary to comply with fair housing laws and obtain the potential client's acknowledgment and agreement. The agent should make it clear that the agent will

> ▸ reject the use of terms indicating race, religion, creed, color, national origin, sex, handicap, age or familial status to describe prospective buyers.

> ▸ terminate the listing if the seller uses race, religion, creed, color, national origin, sex, handicap, age, or familial status in the consideration of an offer.

> ▸ inform the broker if the seller makes any attempt to discriminate illegally.

Offers. A seller cannot refuse to sell a property to an individual based on the individual's belonging to a protected class, and if this is attempted, the real estate professional must not be involved. If the seller asks about the color, religion, creed, national origin, ethnicity, age, or familial status of a buyer, the agent must explain that it is illegal to give out such information. The best risk reduction procedure is to treat all buyers and sellers equally, showing no preference for one over another.

Antitrust

Antitrust laws forbid brokers to band together to set a price on their services in listing and selling property. Even being overheard discussing commission rates or being present at such a conversation can lead to charges of **price fixing**.

The law recognizes that some cooperative arrangements between firms – such as joint development projects – may help consumers by allowing these firms to compete more effectively against each other. Even so the government does not prosecute all agreements between companies, but only those that will raise prices for the public or deny the public new and better products.

Sherman Antitrust Act. The **Sherman Antitrust Act** makes illegal all contracts, agreements, and conspiracies among competitors that would unfairly restrict interstate trade by fixing prices, rigging bids, or other means. An unlawful monopoly is created when one company becomes the only supplier of a product or service by getting rid of competition via secret agreements with other companies.

Clayton Act. The **Clayton Act** prohibits mergers or acquisitions that are likely to lessen competition and increase prices to consumers. The Act also prohibits certain other business practices that under certain circumstances may harm competition. Private parties injured by an antitrust violation may sue in federal court for three times their actual damages, plus court costs and attorneys' fees.

Federal Trade Commission Act. The **Federal Trade Commission Act** forbids unfair competition in interstate commerce but establishes no criminal penalties.

Enforcement. Federal antitrust laws are enforced in three main ways:

> ▸ the Antitrust Division of the Department of Justice (DOJ) brings criminal and civil enforcement actions

> ▸ the FTC brings civil enforcement actions

> ▸ private parties bring lawsuits claiming damages

To collect evidence, Department of Justice lawyers often work with the Federal Bureau of Investigation (FBI) on court-authorized searches of a business, monitoring phone calls and employing informants equipped with secret listening devices.

State attorneys general may sue under the Clayton Act on behalf of injured consumers in their states, and groups of consumers often bring lawsuits on their own.

Anyone associated with an organization found guilty of an antitrust violation and determined to have had knowledge of that violation may also suffer legal consequences.

Penalties. Penalties for Violation of Antitrust Laws include:

> ▸ fines for individuals and corporations, as well as possible imprisonment.

► Under the Clayton Antitrust Act, parties can sue antitrust violators and recover three times the damages they incurred plus court costs and attorneys' fees.

Rules and regulations

State real estate laws and commissioners' rules and regulations attempt to cover every possible risky situation. Non-compliance poses a direct threat to the legal and financial status of licensee and license in the following general ways:

► license expiration
► license revocation or suspension
► licensee discipline
► suit for damages

License expiration. Licenses expire because licensees neglect to:

► maintain E & O insurance when required
► meet education requirements
► observe correct renewal procedures

License revocation or suspension. Licenses are typically revoked or suspended when a licensee is found guilty of:

► obtaining a license under false pretenses
► committing a "prohibited act"
► neglecting to present every written offer as required
► neglecting to deliver signed copies of accepted offers to transaction parties as required
► failing to make sure that all required terms and conditions are present in a contract to purchase
► handling earnest money and other escrow funds improperly

Licensee discipline. A state real estate commission may assess a civil penalty for violations of a statute, rule, or order. Licensees are disciplined for:

► acting without a license when a license is required
► demanding a referral fee without reasonable cause
► entering into a net listing
► trying to induce another licensee's client to end or change an existing agency contract
► paying a commission to an unlicensed individual or company
► receiving an illegal referral fee, rebate or kickback
► practicing with an expired license

Licensee lawsuits. A licensee may be sued by the Department of Justice, Federal Trade Commission, a state real estate commission, a human rights commission, another licensee or firm, or an individual consumer. Licensees are mainly sued for:

► fair housing violations
► antitrust violations
► license law and other state law violations
► breach of contract

- ▸ agency duty violations
- ▸ illegal practice of law
- ▸ failures to disclose
- ▸ customer or client dissatisfaction
- ▸ fraud
- ▸ theft

Misrepresentation

Misrepresentation may be unintentional or intentional.

Unintentional misrepresentation. This type of misrepresentation occurs when a licensee _unknowingly_ conveys inaccurate information to a consumer concerning a property, financing or agency service. False or inaccurate information that the licensee, as a professional, should have known to be false or inaccurate may be included in the definition. Those found guilty generally have to pay fines and may be disciplined by state real estate regulators and professional organizations.

Risky areas for unintentional misrepresentation include:

- ▸ making and reporting measurements
- ▸ describing property
- ▸ offering opinions about future growth and development of a neighborhood or neighboring property
- ▸ making declarative statements about the presence or absence of hazardous materials

The risks of unintentional misrepresentation are reduced if an agent

- ▸ learns to measure and calculate areas accurately
- ▸ relies on measurements reported by others only with extreme caution and specific disclaimers
- ▸ refrains from exaggeration
- ▸ avoids stating opinions a consumer might take for expertise

Intentional misrepresentation. Also known as fraud, this kind of misrepresentation occurs when a licensee _knowingly_ conveys false information about a property, financing or service. Fraud is a criminal act that may result in fines and incarceration, in addition to discipline from state regulators and professional organizations.

Recommending providers

There are several risks attending the recommendation of vendors and service providers to a consumer. First, the consumer may not be satisfied with the performance of the recommended party and blame the licensee. Second, in cases where a recommended provider performs illegal acts, there may be legal consequences for the licensee. Third, if a licensee has a business relationship with a recommended vendor or provider and neglects to disclose the fact, there are license violation consequences.

The major risk management technique is to shift the responsibility for choosing a vendor to the consumer. This can be done by refusing to recommend vendors at all; by presenting a broad range of choices and allowing the consumer to select; or by presenting a short list of thoroughly vetted vendors and allowing the consumer to make the decision, always with the disclaimer that *to the best of the licensee's knowledge*, the vendors on the list are competent and honest, but that the consumer is responsible for investigating and making his or her own judgment before hiring or buying.

Financing and closing

In the financing and closing phases of a transaction, a consumer may feel that a licensee has been incompetent or misleading. Licensees have an obligation to inform and educate their clients throughout the transaction process. Surprises and accusations of incompetence or misrepresentation are among possible results of failing to keep the party informed.

Discrimination. Of course, it is important to comply with relevant laws. Licensees must be mindful of the requirements of ECOA and refrain from participating in any manner of discriminatory lending. It is illegal to:

- ▶ threaten, coerce, intimidate or interfere with a person who is exercising a fair housing right or assisting another other to exercise that right.

- ▶ indicate a limitation or preference based on race, color, national origin, religion, sex, familial status, or handicap in any advertisement or communication. Single-family and owner-occupied housing that is otherwise exempt from the Fair Housing Act is subject to this prohibition against discriminatory advertising.

Progress reporting. All inspections and tests must comply with local and state laws and with the purchase contract. Progress reports should be accurate, timely, in writing, and free of speculation. If a consumer has a question about the meaning of something in an inspection report, the licensee should refer the consumer to the person who wrote the report rather than trying to explain it. This method transfers some of the risk inherent in interpreting the report.

Qualifying buyers. Many transactions fail because a buyer has been improperly qualified before the offer is presented. Using a lender to qualify the buyer saves time and protects the agent against leading a seller to believe a purchaser is fully qualified when this may not be the case. Also, lenders and loan agents are better able to look into the buyer's qualifications than a real estate licensee is. If it becomes necessary to show a property to a potential buyer who has not been qualified by a lender, the licensee can gain some protection by performing an informal qualification and documenting the fact that it was based on the information provided by the buyer. The buyer's signature on this documentation indicates the buyer's acceptance of at least partial responsibility for the qualification.

Lending fees disclosure. The licensee should explain loan fees, charges,

amounts, timing, and responsibilities. Agents can assist in the loan decision by explaining how to compare loans with differing charges and interest rates. The fact that a high origination fee and points may make a loan with a low interest rate unattractive to a borrower is important information for the agent to provide, and providing it may protect the agent against a later complaint that the buyer suffered a loss because of the agent's failure to inform.

Appraisal problems. Delays and appraised value are the typical problem areas. Failure to inform parties about delays can compromise the transaction. An under-appraisal will require the buyer to make a larger down payment or the seller to lower the price. If the property appraises for more than the purchase price, the seller may blame the agent for suggesting the lower price. In such a case, the seller's agent's defense is that the seller agreed to the listing price and that the price was a factor in attracting the buyer to the property.

RESPA Violations. The **Real Estate Settlement Procedures Act (RESPA)** stipulates that the parties to certain purchase transactions must be given accurate information reflecting their closing costs. It also prohibits certain business practices that are not considered to be in the consumer's best interest.

The licensee's risks regarding RESPA primarily relate to

> ▸ failing to ensure that the consumer is informed about his or her rights under the law
>
> ▸ giving or receiving an illegal kickback.

RESPA currently requires lenders to:

> ▸ give a copy of a Consumer Financial Protection Bureau loan information booklet to the applicant. The booklet explains RESPA provisions, general settlement costs, and the required **Closing Disclosure** form. The lender must provide the estimate of closing costs within three business days following the borrower's application.
>
> ▸ give the applicant a Loan Estimate (Form H-24) of expected closing costs within three business days of receiving the application. Actual closing costs may not vary from the estimate beyond certain limits.
>
> ▸ give the buyer the Closing Disclosure (Form H-25) specifying costs to be paid by buyer and seller at closing three business days before consummation.
>
> ▸ give the *buyer* the opportunity to review the final settlement statement *one business day prior to closing*.

RESPA specifically *prohibits* any fee or kickback paid to a party for a service when the party has not actually rendered the service. For example, it is prohibited for an insurance company to pay a real estate agent or a lender for referring a client.

Fees for referring clients to the following services are strictly forbidden:

> ▸ title services (search, insurance)

- ▸ appraisals
- ▸ inspections
- ▸ surveys
- ▸ loan issue
- ▸ credit report
- ▸ attorney services

The sharing of commissions and the payment of referral fees among cooperating brokers and multiple-listing services are not RESPA violations.

Trust fund handling

State laws prescribe how licensees must handle any escrow or earnest money deposits they receive. Those laws usually state that a broker must hold money received in connection with the purchase or lease of real property in a trust fund account. The type of account and financial depository are specified. The broker must record receipt of the money and place that money in the trust account within a specified time period. Usually, the law allows the broker to hold an earnest money check uncashed until the offer is accepted, provided the buyer gives written permission and the seller is informed.

Typical trust fund handling requirements include:

- ▸ the broker named as trustee of the account
- ▸ a federally-insured bank or recognized depository located in the state
- ▸ an account that is not interest-bearing if the financial institution ever requires prior written notice for withdrawals
- ▸ maintenance of records in a particular accounting format
- ▸ separate records kept for each beneficiary, property, or transaction
- ▸ records of funds received and paid out regularly reconciled with bank statements
- ▸ withdrawals only by the broker-trustee or other specifically authorized person

Commingling and conversion. Mixing of personal or company funds with client funds is grounds for the revocation or suspension of a real estate license. Depositing client funds in a personal or business account, or using them for any purpose other than the client's business, is also grounds for suspension or revocation of a license. It is important for the broker to remove commissions, fees or other income earned by the broker from a trust account within the period specified by law to avoid committing an act of commingling.

Check Your Understanding Quiz:

Chapter 7: Risk Management

Carefully read each question and provide your best answer based on what you learned in this module. Then check your answers against the Answer Key which immediately follows the quiz questions.

1. Which of the following is NOT considered a risk management strategy?

   a. Avoidance of risk
   b. Ignoring risk
   c. Transference of risk
   d. Retention of risk

2. Experience has shown that the most practical strategies for risk management in real estate practice are

   a. reduction and transference.
   b. reduction and retention.
   c. avoidance and transference.
   d. reduction and retention.

3. What is considered the first line of defense against risk?

   a. Competence
   b. Communication
   c. Hazard insurance
   d. Education

4. From the standpoint of transparency, state license laws provide for

   a. a maximum limit on broker fees.
   b. a modicum of required disclosures to enhance client and customer awareness.
   c. requirements for licensees to carry E&O insurance.
   d. requirements for a complete transcript of every licensee/client telephone conversation.

5. Which of the following is NOT a disclosure typically required of a real estate licensee?

   a. A disclosure regarding the licensee's previous work experience.
   b. A disclosure regarding agency relationships.
   c. A disclosure regarding the licensee's duties.
   d. A disclosure regarding the condition of the property.

6. Professional liability insurance, a.k.a. Errors and Omissions insurance, protects against two general forms of malpractice. These are which of the following?

    a. Legal and regulatory non-compliance.
    b. Misdemeanors and felonies.
    c. Unprofessional conduct and breach of contract.
    d. Unprofessional conduct and criminal activity.

7. When preparing a comparative market analysis, a licensee should avoid using words such as

    a. "listing price".
    b. "appraisal" and "value".
    c. "estimate".
    d. "approximately".

8. The Real Estate Settlement Procedures Act (RESPA) requires lenders to give a loan applicant a(n)

    a. property condition disclosure.
    b. agency disclosure.
    c. Consumer Financial Protection Bureau information booklet.
    d. copy of their Mortgage Loan Originator license.

9. Real estate broker Cesar has an arrangement with a lender where Cesar gives the lender a $250 referral for every potential client referred by the lender who signs a brokerage agreement. This arrangement

    a. violates the Truth in Lending Act.
    b. violates RESPA.
    c. does not violate any law, it is a good way to build business.
    d. is legal if allowed by the state.

10. One consequence of risk avoidance is that

    a. a licensee will miss the opportunity to benefit from the avoided activity.
    b. a licensee will never be exposed to liability.
    c. a licensee will have an excellent reputation in the real estate community.
    d. a licensee will not be required to carry E&O insurance.

11. Which of the following is a common example of risk transference?

    a. Intensified education
    b. Enhanced safety precautions
    c. Disclosure denial
    d. E&O Insurance

12. Harry, a real estate salesperson at Down-n-Out Realty, had a tough time with a transaction and made several significant mistakes that cost the client approximately $250,000. Who is liable to the client for those damages?

    a. Harry
    b. Harry's broker
    c. Harry and Harry's broker
    d. Harry, Harry's broker, and the client

13. Which of the following is NOT a commonly required disclosure for real estate licensees?

    a. Agency relationships
    b. Duties of a real estate license
    c. The licensee's liability insurance portfolio
    d. Personal interest in the transaction

14. Real estate licensees should

    a. only keep communication records specifically required by the regulatory agency.
    b. not keep records of communications to avoid being caught saying something that is wrong.
    c. keep records of communications.
    d. only communicate in a written form.

15. A standard E&O policy covers

    a. damages resulting from any negligent act, error or omission arising out of Professional Services.
    b. damages resulting from unintentional violations of law.
    c. damages resulting from a negligent act or an antitrust violation.
    d. damages resulting from a negligent act or Fair a Housing Act violation.

Answer Key:

Chapter 7: Risk Management

1. b. Ignoring risk

2. a. reduction and transference.

3. d. Education

4. b. a modicum of required disclosures to enhance client and customer awareness.

5. a. A disclosure regarding the licensee's previous work experience.

6. c. Unprofessional conduct and breach of contract.

7. b. "appraisal" and "value".

8. c. Consumer Financial Protection Bureau information booklet.

9. b. violates RESPA.

10. a. a licensee will miss the opportunity to benefit from the avoided activity.

11. d. E&O Insurance

12. c. Harry and Harry's broker

13. c. The licensee's liability insurance portfolio

14. c. keep records of communications.

15. a. damages resulting from any negligent act, error or omission arising out of Professional Services.

EXERCISE WORKSHOP 2 – NEVADA REAL ESTATE AGENCY

(Chapters 4-7)

I. Progress Checkpoints: Nevada Real Estate Agency

Carefully read each question then provide your best answer based on what you learned in this chapter. Then check your answers against the Answer Key which immediately follows the chapter questions.

1. A Nevada licensee owes certain duties to a client. One of these is to carry out the terms of the brokerage agreement. Name three additional duties.

    1. _____

    2. _____

    3. _____

2. Explain, briefly, by giving an example, (you can make up your own example) how an implied real estate agency could be created.

_____

_____

_____

_____

3. Identify the three types of real estate agency recognized in Nevada.

    1. _____

    2. _____

    3. _____

4. Explain at least two differences between an exclusive brokerage agreement and an open brokerage agreement.

    1. _____

    2. _____

5. Identify the parties to a brokerage agreement.

_____

6. What are the four requirements, in Nevada, for an exclusive agency brokerage agreement?

    1. _____

    2. _____

    3. _____

    4. _____

7. To whom does a Nevada real estate licensee owe a duty of confidentiality?

_____

8. For a Nevada real estate licensee to represent the buyer in the seller the same transaction what form must be completed and signed by the buyer and seller?

    _____

9. What disclosure form is required in Nevada in all real estate transactions in which at least one of the parties is represented by a real estate licensee?

_____

10. What is the only duty owed by a Nevada real estate licensee the client and broker can waive?

_____

11. In Nevada is a brokerage agreement required to be in writing?

    YES _____   NO _____

12. List at least 3 ways an agency agreement can be terminated.

   1. _____

   2. _____

   3. _____

13. In what type of Nevada real estate agency is an "ethical wall" used?

   _____

I. Progress Checkpoints: Nevada Real Estate Agency: Answer Key

1. A Nevada licensee owes certain duties to a client. One of these is to carry out the terms of the brokerage agreement. Name three additional duties.

A duty

   1. **of confidentiality.**

   2. **to disclose material facts which the licensee knows concerning the transaction.**

   3. **to present all offers made by or to the client.**

2. Explain, briefly, by giving an example, (you can make up your own example) how an implied real estate agency could be created.

Broker Bob met a prospective buyer client, Alexandra, at his office. Alexandra gave Bob a list of 6 houses in which she was interested. They both had time available, so Bob showed her all 3 houses on the list, plus a house Bob had listed that was not on Alexandra's list. After they viewed each house Bob commented on the physical condition of the property and rendered his opinion on the asking price. They agreed to meet the next day to view the other three houses on Alexandra's list.

Alexandra did not expressly ask Bob to represent her, and Bob did not expressly agree to represent Alexandra so there is no express agency relationship. However, Bob's conduct, especially commenting on the price and condition of each house could easily lead a reasonable person to believe that Bob has undertaken representation and therefore there was an implied agency relationship.

3. Identify the three types of real estate agency recognized in Nevada.

   1. **Single agency**

   2. **Multiple representation a.k.a. dual agency**

   3. **Assigned agency**

4. Explain at least two differences between an exclusive brokerage agreement and an open brokerage agreement.

   1. **With an exclusive brokerage agreement the client can only retain one broker.**

   2. **With an exclusive brokerage agreement the broker, to earn compensation, is not required to be the procuring cause of a purchase or sale.**

5. Identify the parties to a brokerage agreement.

   The parties to a brokerage agreement are the broker and a client. Even if an affiliated licensee obtained the brokerage agreement on behalf of the broker, the affiliated license is not a party to the agreement.

6. What are the four requirements, in Nevada, for an exclusive agency brokerage agreement?

   1. The contract must be in writing.

   2. The contract must be signed by all parties.

   3. The contract must have definite termination date.

   4. The contract cannot have an automatic renewal clause.

7. To whom does a Nevada real estate licensee owe a duty of confidentiality?

Only to a client.

8. For a Nevada real estate licensee to represent the buyer in the seller the same transaction what form must be completed and signed by the buyer and seller?

Consent to Act

9. What disclosure form is required in Nevada in all real estate transactions in which at least one of the parties is represented by a real estate licensee?

Duties owed by a Nevada Real Estate Licensee

10. What is the only duty owed by a Nevada real estate licensee the client and broker can waive?

   The duty to present all offers.

11. In Nevada is a brokerage agreement required to be in writing?

   YES _____   **NO X**

12. List at least 3 ways and agency agreement can be terminated.

   1. Fulfillment of the purpose

   2. Mutual agreement

   3. Breach of duty by either party

13. In what type of Nevada real estate agency is an "ethical wall" used?

   Assigned agency

II. Applied Practices Exercises – Nevada Real Estate Agency

Exercise 1: Dual Agency

Synopsis: Dual Agency Benefits & Detriments

Representing the buyer and seller in the same transaction is controversial because of the inherent conflict of interest. This situation is often called "dual agency", but the Nevada Real Estate Division prefers the term "multiple representation." The purpose of this exercise is to identify the benefits and detriments of dual agency/multiple representation from the perspective of a client and a licensee.

Instructions:

Complete the table below by identifying the benefits and detriments of dual agency/multiple representation. Develop your answers from the text, your experience, and your independent research. When you have identified several points for each box, review the possible answers provided which follow.

MULTIPLE REPRESENTATION ACTING FOR MORE THAN ONE PARTY TO A TRANSACTION		
	Benefit	**Detriment**
Client		
Broker/licensee		

Exercise 1: De-brief answers / solutions / recommendations

DUAL AGENCY/MULTIPLE REPRESENTATION ACTING FOR MORE THAN ONE PARTY TO A TRANSACTION		
	Benefit	**Detriment**
Client	• Possibly lower commission. • For buyer dual agent will usually have more information about the property.	• Conflict of interest: how can agent be loyal to both parties?
Broker/licensee	• $ Collect fee for both sides of the transaction. $ • Smoother, more efficient transaction.	• Conflict of interest: duty to disclose to one client might conflict with duty of confidentiality to other client.

Exercise 2: Consent to Act form explanation

Synopsis:

Because of the inherent conflict in a dual agency/multiple representation Nevada requires a special disclosure and authorization form, the *Consent to Act* form, before a licensee and broker can represent both clients. The purpose of this assignment is to draft a script that can be used to explain the *Consent to Act* form to both clients.

Instructions:

Write a script that can be used **to explain** the *Consent to Act* form. Include an identification of the parties, the information required (what the Consent to Act form is), and why the Nevada Real Estate Division wants you to receive this form

Why the "CONSENT TO ACT FORM?"

_____

_____

_____

_____

_____

Exercise 2: De-brief answers / solutions / recommendations

To the seller: I represent a buyer who is interested in buying your property.

Since I also represent you, that creates what is often called a dual agency.

Before I continue in that capacity, I need to give you information about dual representation and obtain your consent.

The Nevada Real Division has a form called the *Consent to Act* which I have just given you. The *Consent to Act* form asks you to acknowledge receiving the information and give informed consent.

Do you have any questions about dual agency that I can help you with before you can provide your consent?

Exercise 3: Assigned Agency

Synopsis: Assigned Agency

Assume Nevada enacted a new law which requires real estate licensees to explain assigned agency and get client approval. The purpose of this exercise is to identify what an explanation of assigned agency would look like in your own words. The form must be clear and concise since you will be giving it to prospective clients.

Instructions:

Create a form that could be used to explain an assigned agency to a client.

Exercise narrative: (case story / situation / data)

Nevada does not currently require any special disclosure or client consent to create an assigned agency. Assume you are in a brokerage situation where it has become necessary to create a compliant assigned agency relationship with your client. Further, the client must acknowledge your disclosure and consent to its provisions.

Exercise activities/assignments and responses: (challenges, questions, actions required; participant answers)

In the space provided below, outline in detail what you would suggest as a standardized form to explain and obtain approval of an assigned agency. Include what assigned agency is, how it works, and what choices you have in moving forward. When you have completed your draft, review the proposed form provided which follows.

ASSIGNED AGENCY DISCLOSURE AND CONSENT FORM

_____

_____

_____

_____

_____

_____

_____

_____

_____

_____

Exercise 3: De-brief answers / solutions / recommendations

ASSIGNED AGENCY FORM

Brokerage firm: _____

Broker: _____

Salesperson or Broker-Salesperson: _____

WHAT IS AN ASSIGNED AGENCY?

- Broker represents buyer and seller in same transaction
- Broker assigns separate licensees to represent the buyer and seller
- Licensees operate like single agents
- Confidential information disclosed to broker only
- Example of confidential information: illness reason for selling or buying

CLIENT CHOICES

- Consent
- Reject find own agent
- Reject and represent self
- Ask for assignment to someone else

ACKNOWLEDGEMENT OF RECEIPT OF DISCLOSURE AND CONSENT

	Receipt	Consent	
		Yes	No
Buyer: _____	☐	☐	☐

Seller: _____

Exercise 4: Exclusive Right to Sell

Exercise 4 Synopsis: In this exercise you will develop a completed Exclusive Right to Sell listing form from a narrative of fictional case data.

Exercise 4 Instructions: Read the case data which follows. Then, using the blank Exclusive Right to Sell form provided, complete the form using the narrative data. When you have completed the exercise review the completed form provided immediately following. In completing the form, do not leave any blanks. If a term does not apply put "N/A".

Exercise 4 Narrative data:

On November 1, 2021, Broker Bob, the Broker for We Sell Em Fast, and Sally Seller have agreed to enter an Exclusive Right to Sell Agreement pursuant to the following terms and conditions. Seller: Sally Seller

- Broker: Broker Bob
- Broker Bob address: 4321 Easy Dr., Bliss, NV 89xxx ph. 555-555-5554, email Bob@wesellfast.com
- No salesperson involved
- APN xxx-xx-xxx
- Residential property
- Property and seller address: 1234 Wonderful Lane, Bliss, NV 89xxx ph. 555-555-5555 email Sally@seller.com
- Term of agreement November 1, 2021 – January 31, 2022
- Price $540,000, cash to seller
- Broker compensation 5%
- Selling broker compensation 2%
- Broker entitled to fee if property is sold within 30 days after termination if buyer on list submitted within 10 days after termination.
- Seller acknowledges fee to selling broker
- Seller agrees to pay for resale package
- Seller is not a foreign person
- Property is not under a Property Management Agreement
- Seller has loan with We Finance Them, Loan # 1234
- Seller agrees that listing will be filed with MLS
- Seller does not want any restrictions on Internet advertising.

Blank Exclusive Right to Sell Contract

EXCLUSIVE RIGHT TO SELL CONTRACT

1 All the undersigned SELLER(s), _____ ,
2 and _____
3 hereby irrevocably GRANT(s) _____
4 the Broker, the EXCLUSIVE AUTHORIZATION and RIGHT TO SELL the real Property situated in or near the City of
5 _____ County of _____ , State of Nevada,
6 described as _____
7 APN _____ , for a period commencing, _____ (listing date) and
8 expiring midnight of _____ .
9
10 If checked, the following addendum is attached and becomes part of this Agreement:
11 ❏ Coming Soon Authorization Form. SELLER understands that showings and previews are prohibited during Coming Soon
12 status. Offers, however, if any, may be received.
13 OR
14 ❏ Acknowledgement and Authorization to Withhold Listing Form (office exclusive listing). SELLER understands that once
15 the property is publicly marketed, the listing is required to be entered into the MLS within 1 business day.
16
17 This property is ❏ Residential   OR   ❏ Vacant Land   OR   ❏ Multifamily (4 Units or Less)
18
19 **TERMS OF SALE**   SELLER hereby employs Broker as exclusive Licensee to sell the described real Property, fixtures and
20 personal property. SELLER hereby grants Broker the exclusive right to sell for a sale price of
21 $ _____ , on the following terms:
22 _____
23 _____
24 or at such price and terms as shall be acceptable to SELLER. Broker is herein authorized to accept a deposit for any part of the
25 purchase price and hold it in trust or place it in an escrow established for the sale of the subject Property.
26 Broker accepts such employment and agrees to use diligence in procuring a BUYER for the Property.
27
28 **COMPENSATION TO BROKER NOTICE: The amount or rate of real estate commission is not fixed by law. The**
29 **commission is set by each Broker individually and may be negotiable between the SELLER and Broker.**
30 SELLER agrees to pay Broker as compensation for services rendered a fee of $ _____ or _____ percent of the
31 selling price under the following:
32 1. [_____/_____/_____/_____] SELLER(s) acknowledge(s) that from total commission, Listing Broker will offer
33      $ _____ or _____ percent selling price as compensation to Selling Broker. or
34 2. The Property is sold, exchanged or otherwise transferred during the term hereof, by SELLER, or through any other
35   source, **or**
36 3. The Property is transferred, conveyed, leased without the consent of Broker, or made unmarketable by SELLER's
37   voluntary act during the term hereof or any extension thereof, **or**
38 4. A sale, exchange, or other transfer of the Property is made by SELLER within _____ days after the termination of this
39   agreement or any extension thereof, to persons with whom Broker shall have negotiated during the term hereof provided
40   that Broker shall have submitted a notice in writing to SELLER within _____ days of termination of this agreement or
41   any extension thereof. The notice shall contain the name of the prospective BUYER(s), date(s) of negotiation and a brief
42   summary of the negotiations. However, this provision shall not apply if, during the term of said protection period, a valid
43   Exclusive Authorization and Right to Sell agreement is entered into with another licensed real estate Broker.

Property Address _____ .

Page 1 of 4   SELLER(s) [_____/_____/_____/_____] and Licensee [_____] have read this page.   RSAR© 01/21
This copyright protected form was created by and for the use of the members of RSAR and SNR.   ERTS 1/4

1 **BROKER COOPERATION**   SELLER(s) understand(s) that Broker is a member of the Multiple Listing Service (MLS) and
2 a member of the local Association of REALTORS®, and that this listing will be filed with said service within two (2) business
3 days, of listing or signature date whichever is later. SELLER agrees that all members of the Multiple Listing   Service (MLS),
4 and other Brokers, may act in association with Broker in procuring or attempting to procure a BUYER for the Property. In the
5 event a sale or exchange shall be made or a BUYER procured by a member of the Multiple Listing Service (MLS) or another
6 Broker other than Listing Broker, the terms of this agreement shall apply to such transaction, although payment for fee or
7 compensation made hereunder shall be made by SELLER only to Listing Broker. Broker is authorized to cooperate with other
8 Brokers in the marketing and sale or exchange of the Property. It is agreed that such Brokers may act as cooperating Brokers
9 in procuring or attempting to procure a BUYER in accordance with this agreement. In the event of an exchange, Broker is
10 hereby authorized to represent all parties and collect compensation from them, provided there is full disclosure to all
11 principals.
12
13 **SELLER'S OBLIGATIONS AND WARRANTIES**
14 1. SELLER agrees to make available to Broker and prospective Buyers all data, records and documents pertaining to the
15   Property.
16 2. [_____/_____/_____/_____] If the Property is located in a common-interest community, SELLER agrees to
17   provide, at SELLERS expense, the common-interest community documents (Resale Package) as required by Nevada
18   Revised Statutes (NRS). SELLER to order resale package within five (5) days of acceptance of the purchase agreement.
19 3. SELLER agrees to allow Broker, or any other Broker with whom Broker chooses to cooperate, to show the Property at
20   reasonable times and upon reasonable notice.
21 4. SELLER agrees to secure all valuables, including but not limited to pharmaceutical, weapons, jewelry, and any other
22   items of concern.
23 5. SELLER agrees to commit no act which might tend to obstruct the Broker's performance hereunder.
24 6. In the event of a sale, SELLER will promptly, upon Broker's request, deposit in escrow all instruments necessary to
25   complete the sale.
26 7. SELLER agrees to deliver an escrow instruction, irrevocably assigning Broker's compensation in an amount equal to the
27   compensation provided above from SELLER's proceeds at close of escrow.
28 8. Nevada law requires that property owners complete a SELLER'S REAL PROPERTY DISCLOSURE FORM for
29   residential properties of four units or less. Broker authorized to furnish copies to potential BUYER(s).
30 9. SELLER agrees to hold the Broker harmless from any liabilities or damages arising out of incorrect or undisclosed
31   information with respect to the above described Seller's Real Property Disclosure Form. SELLER agrees to notify
32   Broker expeditiously of any changes affecting the marketing of the Property.
33 10. The undersigned SELLER warrants recorded ownership of the Property or the authority to execute this agreement.
34 11. SELLER is aware that listing includes water rights (if applicable), unless SELLER excludes by deed.
35 12. A. [_____/_____/_____] I/we am not a foreign person.
36   OR
37   B. [_____/_____/_____] I/we am a foreign person. The Foreign Investment and Real Property Tax Act
38   requires a BUYER purchasing real property from a foreign person to withhold tax from the sale proceeds unless an
39   exemption applies. SELLER agrees to provide Broker and Escrow Company with (a) Non-Foreign Seller Affidavit, or
40   (b) Withholding Certificate Form from the Internal Revenue Service to consent to withholding of tax from the
41   proceeds of sale as required, unless it is established that the transaction is exempt.
42
43 **PROPERTY UNDER MANAGEMENT/LEASE**
44 Property ❑ is   OR   ❑ is not under a Property Management Agreement.
45 Property ❑ is   OR   ❑ is not Tenant Occupied. If occupied, term of Lease: _____
46 SELLER shall be responsible to notify tenant that the Property is for sale. SELLER shall contact the Property Manager to
47 make arrangements for termination or transfer of tenants' lease and disposition of security deposit. SELLER authorizes Listing
48 Licensee to contact _____(Property Manager) with
49 _____ (Management Company)
50 at _____ (Contact Number). Property Manager has 30-days for reconciliation and
51 disbursement of security deposits and Property is subject to Tenant Rights and/or Property Management Agreement.

Property Address _____.

Page 2 of 4   SELLER(s) [_____/_____/_____/_____] and Licensee [_____] have read this page.   RSAR® 01/21
              This copyright protected form was created by and for the use of the members of RSAR and SNR.   ERTS 2/4

1 SELLER'S INSTRUCTIONS AND AUTHORIZATIONS
2 1. SELLER authorizes Broker to place a "FOR SALE" sign upon the Property.
3 2. SELLER authorizes Broker to install an LOCKBOX upon the Property.
4 3. Evidence of merchantable title shall be in form of policy of title insurance issued by a responsible title company.
5 4. SELLER authorizes Broker to obtain loan information from _____ Loan # _____
6   and from _____ Loan #_____.
7 5. SELLER authorizes Broker to assist in scheduling work to repair or maintain the Property pursuant to NRS 624.031(11).
8   SELLER acknowledges Broker will not receive any additional compensation for providing such assistance.
9 6. SELLER acknowledges any work scheduled by the Broker to repair or maintain the Property during the term of this
10   Agreement must not exceed $10,000 or require a building permit.
11
12 [_____/_____/_____] SELLER(s): Execution of this form confirms that the undersigned SELLER(s) has (have)
13 executed concurrently herewith a Listing Data Input Form and, unless certified in writing, grant(s) consent to inclusion of the
14 information thereon into the Multiple Listing Service. Further, SELLER(s) consent(s) to dissemination of the information
15 through the Multiple Listing Service. The SELLER(s) acknowledge(s) and agrees that all photographs, images, graphics, video
16 recordings, virtual tours, drawings, written descriptions, remarks, narratives, pricing information, and other copyrightable data
17 and information relating to the Property provided by the SELLER(s) to the Broker (the "Seller Listing Content"), or otherwise
18 obtained or produced by the Broker in connection with this Agreement ("the Broker Listing Content"), and any changes to the
19 Seller Listing Content or the Broker Listing Content, may be filed with one or more multiple listing services, including in
20 compilations of listings, and otherwise distributed, publicly displayed and reproduced. SELLER hereby grants to Broker a
21 non-exclusive, irrevocable, worldwide, royalty free license to use, sublicense through multiple tiers, publish, display, and
22 reproduce Seller Listing Content, to prepare derivative works of the Seller Listing Content and to distribute the Seller Listing
23 Content or any derivative works thereof. SELLER represents and warrants to Broker that the Seller Listing Content, and the
24 license granted to Broker for the Seller Listing Content, does not violate or infringe upon the rights, including copyright rights,
25 of any person or entity. SELLER acknowledges and agrees that as between SELLER and Broker, all Broker Listing Content is
26 owned exclusively by the Broker, and SELLER has no right, title or interest in or to any Broker Listing Content.
27 SELLER further understands and acknowledges that the Multiple Listing Service will disseminate the Property's listing
28 information to Internet sites as well as online providers and such sites are generally available to the public. Some of these
29 websites may display an Automated Valuation Model to estimate the market value of the Property or provide a link to the
30 estimate. In addition, some websites may include a Commentary/Review Section (or blog) where consumers may include
31 comments about the Property or provide a link to such comments.
32
33 [_____/_____/_____] Seller wishes the Broker to submit the Property's listing information for
34   *Seller initial*   dissemination to Internet sites with NO RESTRICTIONS.
35   -OR-
36 Seller has the right to opt-out of any of the following by initialing the appropriate space(s):
37 [_____/_____/_____] I/We have elected NOT to display the listed Property on ANY Internet site.
38   *Seller initial*
39 [_____/_____/_____] I/We have elected to WITHHOLD the address of the listing Property from display
40   *Seller initial*   on ANY Internet site
42 [_____/_____/_____] I/We DO NOT want an Automated Valuation displayed or linked to the listed
43   *Seller initial*   Property (consumers may be notified that this feature was disabled at the request of
44   the seller.)
45 [_____/_____/_____] I/We DO NOT want a Commentary/Review Section displayed or linked to the listed
46   *Seller initial*   Property. (consumers may be notified that this feature was disabled at the request of
47   the seller.)
48 SELLER understands and acknowledges that if opting out of display on any Internet site, consumers who conduct searches for
49 listings on the Internet will not see information about this Property in response to their search.
50 Any future Status Change Reports which update, correct, extend or in any way change the information provided by the
51 SELLER's (on the above-mentioned Listing Data Input Form, and are executed by the Seller's), constitute amendments not
52 only to that Listing Data Input Form but to the terms of this Contract as well. Thus, such properly executed Status Change
53 Reports may include, but are not limited to, amendments to the SELLER's selling price of the subject real Property and
54 extensions of the duration of this Contract. Each such Status Change Report shall be attached to this Contract and its terms
55 incorporated herein.

Property Address _____.

Page 3 of 4   SELLER(s) [_____/_____/_____/_____] and Licensee [_____] have read this page.   RSAR© 01/21
                                                                                                                      ERTS 3/4
This copyright protected form was created by and for the use of the members of RSAR and SNR.

1 **PRESENTATION OF OFFERS**   SELLER understands that Broker is obligated to present all offers until the close of
2 escrow. SELLER is advised to seek legal counsel prior to acceptance of a subsequent offer, unless the subsequent offer is
3 contingent upon the termination of an existing contract.
4
5 **SECURITY DEVICES**   If property is equipped with security cameras or similar devices that are capable of audio
6 recordings or broadcasts, SELLER must notify any prospective buyer, broker, or other party touring the property. If SELLER
7 has any questions about the requirements of NRS 200.650, SELLER is advised to seek legal counsel.
8
9 **EQUAL HOUSING OPPORTUNITY**   This Property is offered in compliance with federal, state and local
10 antidiscrimination laws.
11
12 **MUTUAL AGREEMENTS**   If suit is brought to collect the compensation or if Broker successfully defends any action
13 brought against Broker by SELLER relating to this authorization or under any sales agreement relating to the Property,
14 SELLER agrees to pay all costs incurred by Broker in connection with such action, including a reasonable attorney's fee.
15
16 **PROFESSIONAL CONSULTATION ADVISORY**   A real estate Broker is qualified to advise on real estate. The
17 SELLERS are advised to consult with appropriate professionals, including but not limited to, engineers, surveyors, appraisers,
18 lawyers, CPAs, or other professionals, on specific topics, including but not limited to, legal, tax, water rights and other
19 consequences of the sale of the Property.
20
21 **CODE OF ETHICS**   Not all real estate licensees are REALTORS(S)®.   A REALTOR® is a member of the National
22 Association of REALTORS® and therefore subscribes to a higher ethical standard in the industry, the REALTOR® Code of
23 Ethics. To receive a copy of the REALTOR® Code of Ethics, ask your real estate professional or the local Association of
24 REALTORS®.
25
26 **ADDITIONAL LISTING TERMS** _____
27 _____
28
29 If this property is a Short Sale or becomes a Short Sale, SELLER, is advised to consult appropriate professionals.
30
31 SELLER _____   Dated _____
32
33 SELLER _____   Dated _____
34
35 SELLER _____   Dated _____
36
37 SELLER _____   Dated _____
38
39 Address _____   Phone _____   Fax _____
40
42 City/State/Zip _____   Email _____
43
44 Listing Office _____   Phone _____   Fax _____
45
46 Address _____   Email _____
47
48 City/State/Zip _____
49
50 Licensee Name _____   Licensee Nevada License # _____
51
52 Licensee Signature _____   Dated _____

Completed Exclusive Right to Sell Contract

EXCLUSIVE RIGHT TO SELL CONTRACT

1 All the undersigned SELLER(s), Sally Seller _____ ,
2 and _____
3 hereby irrevocably GRANT(s) Broker Bob _____
4 the Broker, the EXCLUSIVE AUTHORIZATION and RIGHT TO SELL the real Property situated in or near the City of
5 Bliss _____ County of Euphoria _____ , State of Nevada,
6 described as 1234 Wonderful Lane, 89xxx _____
7 APN xxx-xx-xxx _____ , for a period commencing, November 21, 2021 _____ (listing date) and
8 expiring midnight of January 31, 2022 _____ .
9
10 If checked, the following addendum is attached and becomes part of this Agreement:
11 ❏ Coming Soon Authorization Form. SELLER understands that showings and previews are prohibited during Coming Soon
12 status. Offers, however, if any, may be received.
13 OR
14 ❏ Acknowledgement and Authorization to Withhold Listing Form (office exclusive listing). SELLER understands that once
15 the property is publicly marketed, the listing is required to be entered into the MLS within 1 business day.
16
17 This property is ☑Residential   OR   ❏ Vacant Land   OR   ❏ Multifamily (4 Units or Less)
18
19 **TERMS OF SALE**   SELLER hereby employs Broker as exclusive Licensee to sell the described real Property, fixtures and
20 personal property. SELLER hereby grants Broker the exclusive right to sell same for the price of
21 $ $540,000 _____ , on the following terms:
22 Cash to seller _____
23 _____
24 or at such price and terms as shall be acceptable to SELLER. Broker is herein authorized to accept a deposit for any part of the
25 purchase price and hold it in trust or place it in an escrow established for the sale of the subject Property.
26 Broker accepts such employment and agrees to use diligence in procuring a BUYER for the Property.
27
28 **COMPENSATION TO BROKER NOTICE: The amount or rate of real estate commission is not fixed by law. The**
29 **commission is set by each Broker individually and may be negotiable between the SELLER and Broker.**
30 SELLER agrees to pay Broker as compensation for services rendered a fee of $ _____ or ⁵____ percent of the
31 selling price under the following:
32   1. [SS __/____/____/____ SELLER(s) acknowledge(s) that from total commission, Listing Broker will offer
33      $ _____ or ² ____ percent selling price as compensation to Selling Broker. **or**
34   2. The Property is sold, exchanged or otherwise transferred during the term hereof, by SELLER, or through any other
35   source, **or**
36   3. The Property is transferred, conveyed, leased without the consent of Broker, or made unmarketable by SELLER's
37   voluntary act during the term hereof or any extension thereof, **or**
38   4. A sale, exchange, or other transfer of the Property is made by SELLER within ³⁰____ days after the termination of this
39   agreement or any extension thereof, to persons with whom Broker shall have negotiated during the term hereof provided
40   that Broker shall have submitted a notice in writing to SELLER within ¹⁰____ days of termination of this agreement or
41   any extension thereof. The notice shall contain the name of the prospective BUYER(s), date(s) of negotiation and a brief
42   summary of the negotiations. However, this provision shall not apply if, during the term of said protection period, a valid
43   Exclusive Authorization and Right to Sell agreement is entered into with another licensed real estate Broker.

Property Address 1234 Wonderful Lane _____ .

Page 1 of 4   SELLER(s) [SS _____/_____/_____/_____] and Licensee [BB _____] have read this page.   RSAR# 01/21
This copyright protected form was created by and for the use of the members of RSAR and SNR.   ERTS 1/4

1 BROKER COOPERATION   SELLER(s) understand(s) that Broker is a member of the Multiple Listing Service (MLS) and
2 a member of the local Association of REALTORS®, and that this listing will be filed with said service within two (2) business
3 days, of listing or signature date whichever is later. SELLER agrees that all members of the Multiple Listing   Service (MLS),
4 and other Brokers, may act in association with Broker in procuring or attempting to procure a BUYER for the Property. In the
5 event a sale or exchange shall be made or a BUYER procured by a member of the Multiple Listing Service (MLS) or another
6 Broker other than Listing Broker, the terms of this agreement shall apply to such transaction, although payment for fee or
7 compensation made hereunder shall be made by SELLER only to Listing Broker. Broker is authorized to cooperate with other
8 Brokers in the marketing and sale or exchange of the Property. It is agreed that such Brokers may act as cooperating Brokers
9 in procuring or attempting to procure a BUYER in accordance with this agreement. In the event of an exchange, Broker is
10 hereby authorized to represent all parties and collect compensation from them, provided there is full disclosure to all
11 principals.
12
13 **SELLER'S OBLIGATIONS AND WARRANTIES**
14 1. SELLER agrees to make available to Broker and prospective Buyers all data, records and documents pertaining to the
15   Property.
16 2. [SS /_____/_____/_____] If the Property is located in a common-interest community, SELLER agrees to
17   provide, at SELLERS expense, the common-interest community documents (Resale Package) as required by Nevada
18   Revised Statutes (NRS). SELLER to order resale package within five (5) days of acceptance of the purchase agreement.
19 3. SELLER agrees to allow Broker, or any other Broker with whom Broker chooses to cooperate, to show the Property at
20   reasonable times and upon reasonable notice.
21 4. SELLER agrees to secure all valuables, including but not limited to pharmaceuticals, weapons, jewelry, and any other
22   items of concern.
23 5. SELLER agrees to commit no act which might tend to obstruct the Broker's performance hereunder.
24 6. In the event of a sale, SELLER will promptly, upon Broker's request, deposit in escrow all instruments necessary to
25   complete the sale.
26 7. SELLER agrees to deliver an escrow instruction, irrevocably assigning Broker's compensation in an amount equal to the
27   compensation provided above from SELLER's proceeds at close of escrow.
28 8. Nevada law requires that property owners complete a SELLER'S REAL PROPERTY DISCLOSURE FORM for
29   residential properties of four units or less. Broker authorized to furnish copies to potential BUYER(s).
30 9. SELLER agrees to hold the Broker harmless from any liabilities or damages arising out of incorrect or undisclosed
31   information with respect to the above described Seller's Real Property Disclosure Form. SELLER agrees to notify
32   Broker expeditiously of any changes affecting the marketing of the Property.
33 10. The undersigned SELLER warrants recorded ownership of the Property or the authority to execute this agreement.
34 11. SELLER is aware that listing includes water rights (if applicable), unless SELLER excludes by deed.
35 12. A. [SS /_____/_____/_____] I/we am a foreign person.
36   OR
37   B. [_____/_____/_____] I/we am a foreign person. The Foreign Investment and Real Property Tax Act
38   requires a BUYER purchasing real property from a foreign person to withhold tax from the sale proceeds unless an
39   exemption applies. SELLER agrees to provide Broker and Escrow Company with (a) Non-Foreign Seller Affidavit, or
40   (b) Withholding Certificate Form from the Internal Revenue Service to consent to withholding of tax from the
41   proceeds of sale as required, unless it is established that the transaction is exempt.
42
43 **PROPERTY UNDER MANAGEMENT/LEASE**
44 Property ☐ is   OR ☑ is not under a Property Management Agreement.
45 Property ☐ is   OR ☐ is not Tenant Occupied. If occupied, term of Lease: N/A _____
46 SELLER shall be responsible to notify tenant that the Property is for sale. SELLER shall contact the Property Manager to
47 make arrangements for termination or transfer of tenants' lease and disposition of security deposit. SELLER authorizes Listing
48 Licensee to contact N/A _____ (Property Manager) with
49 _____ (Management Company)
50 at _____ (Contact Number). Property Manager has 30-days for reconciliation and
51 disbursement of security deposits and Property is subject to Tenant Rights and/or Property Management Agreement.

Property Address 1234 Wonderful Lane _____ .

Page 2 of 4   SELLER(s) [SS _____/_____/_____/_____] and Licensee [BB _____] have read this page.   RSAR© 01/21
          This copyright protected form was created by and for the use of the members of RSAR and SNR.   ERTS 2/4

1 SELLER'S INSTRUCTIONS AND AUTHORIZATIONS
2 1. SELLER authorizes Broker to place a "FOR SALE" sign upon the Property.
3 2. SELLER authorizes Broker to install an LOCKBOX upon the Property.
4 3. Evidence of merchantable title shall be in form of policy of title insurance issued by a responsible title company.
5 4. SELLER authorizes Broker to obtain loan information from We Finance Them _____ Loan # 1234 _____
6 and from _____ Loan #_____.
7 5. SELLER authorizes Broker to assist in scheduling work to repair or maintain the Property pursuant to NRS 624.031(11).
8 SELLER acknowledges Broker will not receive any additional compensation for providing such assistance.
9 6. SELLER acknowledges any work scheduled by the Broker to repair or maintain the Property during the term of this
10 Agreement must not exceed $10,000 or require a building permit.
11
12 [SS ___/___/___] SELLER(s): Execution of this form confirms that the undersigned SELLER(s) has (have)
13 executed concurrently herewith a Listing Data Input Form and, unless certified in writing, grant(s) consent to inclusion of the
14 information thereon into the Multiple Listing Service. Further, SELLER(s) consent(s) to dissemination of the information
15 through the Multiple Listing Service. The SELLER(s) acknowledge(s) and agrees that all photographs, images, graphics, video
16 recordings, virtual tours, drawings, written descriptions, remarks, narratives, pricing information, and other copyrightable data
17 and information relating to the Property provided by the SELLER(s) to the Broker (the "Seller Listing Content"), or otherwise
18 obtained or produced by the Broker in connection with this Agreement ("the Broker Listing Content"), and any changes to the
19 Seller Listing Content or the Broker Listing Content, may be filed with one or more multiple listing services, including in
20 compilations of listings, and otherwise distributed, publicly displayed and reproduced. SELLER hereby grants to Broker a
21 non-exclusive, irrevocable, worldwide, royalty free license to use, sublicense through multiple tiers, publish, display, and
22 reproduce Seller Listing Content, to prepare derivative works of the Seller Listing Content and to distribute the Seller Listing
23 Content or any derivative works thereof. SELLER represents and warrants to Broker that the Seller Listing Content, and the
24 license granted to Broker for the Seller Listing Content, does not violate or infringe upon the rights, including copyright rights,
25 of any person or entity. SELLER acknowledges and agrees that as between SELLER and Broker, all Broker Listing Content is
26 owned exclusively by the Broker, and SELLER has no right, title or interest in or to any Broker Listing Content.
27 SELLER further understands and acknowledges that the Multiple Listing Service will disseminate the Property's listing
28 information to Internet sites as well as online providers and such sites are generally available to the public. Some of these
29 websites may display an Automated Valuation Model to estimate the market value of the Property or provide a link to the
30 estimate. In addition, some websites may include a Commentary/Review Section (or blog) where consumers may include
31 comments about the Property or provide a link to such comments.
32
33 [SS ___/___/___] Seller wishes the Broker to submit the Property's listing information for
34 Seller initial dissemination to Internet sites with NO RESTRICTIONS.
35 -OR-
36 Seller has the right to opt-out of any of the following by initialing the appropriate space(s):
37 [___/___/___] I/We have elected NOT to display the listed Property on ANY Internet site.
38 Seller initial
39 [___/___/___] I/We have elected to WITHHOLD the address of the listing Property from display
40 Seller initial on ANY Internet site
42 [___/___/___] I/We DO NOT want an Automated Valuation displayed or linked to the listed
43 Seller initial Property (consumers may be notified that this feature was disabled at the request of
44 the seller.)
45 [___/___/___] I/We DO NOT want a Commentary/Review Section displayed or linked to the listed
46 Seller initial Property. (consumers may be notified that this feature was disabled at the request of
47 the seller.)
48 SELLER understands and acknowledges that if opting out of display on any Internet site, consumers who conduct searches for
49 listings on the Internet will not see information about this Property in response to their search.
50 Any future Status Change Reports which update, correct, extend or in any way change the information provided by the
51 SELLER's (on the above-mentioned Listing Data Input Form, and are executed by the Seller's), constitute amendments not
52 only to that Listing Data Input Form but to the terms of this Contract as well. Thus, such properly executed Status Change
53 Reports may include, but are not limited to, amendments to the SELLER's selling price of the subject real Property and
54 extensions of the duration of this Contract. Each such Status Change Report shall be attached to this Contract and its terms
55 incorporated herein.

Property Address 1234 Wonderful Lane _____.

Page 3 of 4   SELLER(s) [SS ___/___/___/___] and Licensee [BB ___] have read this page.   RSAR© 01/21
ERTS 3/4

1 **PRESENTATION OF OFFERS** SELLER understands that Broker is obligated to present all offers until the close of
2 escrow. SELLER is advised to seek legal counsel prior to acceptance of a subsequent offer, unless the subsequent offer is
3 contingent upon the termination of an existing contract.
4
5 **SECURITY DEVICES** If property is equipped with security cameras or similar devices that are capable of audio
6 recordings or broadcasts, SELLER must notify any prospective buyer, broker, or other party touring the property. If SELLER
7 has any questions about the requirements of NRS 200.650, SELLER is advised to seek legal counsel.
8
9 **EQUAL HOUSING OPPORTUNITY** This Property is offered in compliance with federal, state and local
10 antidiscrimination laws.
11
12 **MUTUAL AGREEMENTS** If suit is brought to collect the compensation or if Broker successfully defends any action
13 brought against Broker by SELLER relating to this authorization or under any sales agreement relating to the Property,
14 SELLER agrees to pay all costs incurred by Broker in connection with such action, including a reasonable attorney's fee.
15
16 **PROFESSIONAL CONSULTATION ADVISORY** A real estate Broker is qualified to advise on real estate. The
17 SELLERS are advised to consult with appropriate professionals, including but not limited to, engineers, surveyors, appraisers,
18 lawyers, CPAs, or other professionals, on specific topics, including but not limited to, legal, tax, water rights and other
19 consequences of the sale of the Property.
20
21 **CODE OF ETHICS** Not all real estate licensees are REALTORS)®. A REALTOR® is a member of the National
22 Association of REALTORS® and therefore subscribes to a higher ethical standard in the industry, the REALTOR® Code of
23 Ethics. To receive a copy of the REALTOR® Code of Ethics, ask your real estate professional or the local Association of
24 REALTORS®.
25
26 **ADDITIONAL LISTING TERMS** _____
27 _____
28
29 If this property is a Short Sale or becomes a Short Sale, SELLER, is advised to consult appropriate professionals.
30
31 SELLER **Sally Seller** Dated **11/1/2021**
32
33 SELLER _____ Dated _____
34
35 SELLER _____ Dated _____
36
37 SELLER _____ Dated _____
38
39 Address **1234 Wonderful Lane** Phone **555-555-5555** Fax _____
40
42 City/State/Zip **Bliss, NV 89xxx** Email **Sally@Seller.com**
43
44 Listing Office **We Sell em Fast** Phone **555-555-5554** Fax _____
45
46 Address **4321 Easy Ave** Email **bob@wesellfast.com**
47
48 City/State/Zip **Bliss, NV 89xxx**
49
50 Licensee Name **Broker Bob** Licensee Nevada License # **xxxxx**
51
52 Licensee Signature _____ Dated **11/1/2021**

Property Address **1234 Wonderful Lane** _____.

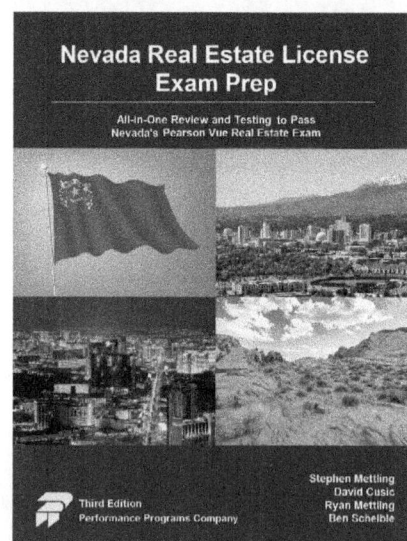

www.ingramcontent.com/pod-product-compliance
Lightning Source LLC
Chambersburg PA
CBHW080551220326
41599CB00032B/6440